Easy Ways to Make Technology Work for You

From Grade Books to Graphic Organizers

by David A. Dockterman, Ed.D.

formerly titled *Weaving Technology Into Your Teaching*
(Published by Tom Snyder Productions)

SCHOLASTIC
PROFESSIONAL BOOKS

NEW YORK • TORONTO • LONDON • AUCKLAND • SYDNEY
MEXICO CITY • NEW DELHI • HONG KONG • BUENOS AIRES

Dedicated to great teachers, great classes,
and the pursuit of great education.

Cover design by Josué Castilleja
Cover art by Mike Moran
Interior art by Jenny Williams

Published by Scholastic Inc.
Printed in the U.S.A.
ISBN 0-439-43761-X

1 2 3 4 5 6 7 8 9 10   40   09 08 07 06 05 04 03

Contents

Introduction:
Technology
in the
Classroom

Technology should be transparent in classrooms, instead of yet another thing that teachers have to manage. They shouldn't be asking themselves "How in the world am I going to cram this into my schedule?" Rather, teachers should continue with the curriculum and teaching methods that have already made them great teachers. Technology should serve as a tool that a teacher can pull out of her pocket and put into use in the classroom. The technology isn't the focus; it's a transparent support for what's happening in the curriculum, and what's happening for the teacher and her students.

Mark Benno
Technology Facilitator
Hillcrest Professional Development School
Waco, Texas

Introduction

Our Nation is at risk. Our once unchallenged preeminence in commerce, industry, science, and technological innovation is being overtaken by competitors throughout the world.[1]

In 1983, a government report called *A Nation at Risk* proclaimed that the educational foundations of our society were being eroded by a "tide of mediocrity." The United States had "squandered" the educational gains made in the 1950s in response to the Soviet launch of Sputnik. Our nation teetered on the edge of losing its economic and educational preeminence in the world. At stake, the report warned, was not just our leadership in commerce but "our very future as a Nation and a people." Something had to be done, and much of the attention focused on the country's schools.

Twenty years later, the United States maintains its role as a world leader, and the spotlight of national attention still shines brightly on our schools. A few vocal critics claim that our public education system, despite all the reform efforts of the 1980s and 90s, is a failure. The public, although more generous, seems to agree with the "mediocre" rating given by the authors of *A Nation at Risk*. A 2001 poll by Phi Delta Kappa and Gallup found that while less than 5% of those surveyed actually gave our nation's public schools a failing grade, only 23% awarded the schools a grade of A or B (and only a small fraction of that 23% gave an A). While respondents generally thought better of their local school systems than they did of the nation's as a whole, it's clear that dissatisfaction remains widespread.[2]

Read a newspaper or magazine headline about education today, and you are bound to see evidence of the latest effort to "fix" our schools: the movement toward student assessment and accountability. Schools, the reasoning goes, haven't responded to the urgent warnings of the last few decades because they haven't needed to. Unless they are held accountable for their product, as businesses are, schools won't change. Consequently, most states have begun to closely measure schools' output in the form of student performance, tracking the rise and fall of all kinds of standardized test scores. Many students are tested annually and the stakes are high. In some states, test scores determine whether a student moves from one grade to the next, or graduates at all. Real estate values in some communities fluctuate based on how well the local schools performed in the most recent statewide examinations. If students don't measure up, they, the schools they go to, and the neighborhoods they live in could all face serious consequences.

In this climate so focused on student performance, I have written a book about technology and *teachers.* Why about teachers and not about students? Schools are wired. Computers are in classrooms. The Internet reaches out to every corner of the nation. Shouldn't I be writing about how students can use these technological advances to enhance their learning and raise their test scores, without the help of the teachers and school systems that have failed them? As someone with a 20-year history in the educational technology industry, shouldn't I be telling you how computers will ride to the rescue of our beleaguered schools and our underperforming children?

Long before computers entered schools, other technologies promised to cure the ills of an ailing educational system.

If I did, I'd be just one more voice in a chorus of educational technology reformers throughout our nation's history. Long before computers entered schools, other technologies promised to cure the ills of an ailing educational system. Early in the 20th century, for example, Thomas Edison touted one of his new inventions as an incredible boon to education. The motion picture, he predicted, "will wipe out narrow-minded prejudices which are founded on ignorance, it will create a feeling of sympathy and a desire to help the downtrodden people of the earth, and it will give new ideals to be followed."[3] Teaching "everything, from mathematics to morality,"[4] motion pictures would entice and engage children while educating them. In fact, a 1919 study at the University of Wisconsin concluded "that a well-constructed film may have as high a teaching efficiency as a very superior teacher or even more."[5]

How would films perform these amazing educational feats? By appealing to what many at the time believed to be the workings of the human mind. "The mind works under laws just as definite," educator Dudley Hays wrote in 1923, "as are the laws of physics." These laws included "the law of habit" and "the law of vividness." Show a vivid image repeatedly to a student, and "the pupil will not fail to grasp it."[6] While we may look back at these scientific "laws" of the early 20th century with a wink and a nod, they came on the heels of incredible advances in science which led many to believe that we truly were on the verge of understanding everything. The newly established science of psychology explored the physical laws of the mind, and provided validation, just as science does today, for bold, new ideas. Educational film enthusiasts used the new research and scientific jargon to promote their message: movies can teach.

In the 1930s, 40s, and 50s, the broadcast technologies of radio and television offered a new vehicle for audio and video education and perpetuated the notion that machines could do the job of teachers. The most ardent supporters of educational radio even predicted that "radio ultimately will be used as a substitute for certain teacher instruction."[7] Since television combined both auditory and visual components, the hopes were even higher for this technology. A 1961 Ford Foundation summary of experiments in educational TV concluded "that students at both the school and college level learn as much — and in some cases significantly more — from televised instruction as from conventional instruction."[8] These results echoed those from the University of Wisconsin in 1919: In many instances, the technology can do the job at least as well as a teacher.

Enter the Computer Age

By the 1960s, though, another technology had emerged on the educational scene. The computer "revolution" in education actually began in the 1950s and 60s with mainframe computer systems that managed units of programmed instruction. These huge, expensive devices promised to individualize education through the magic of programmed teaching and learning. A Republic Steel advertisement from the 1960s illustrates the excitement and high expectations that welcomed these early computers into the schools.

> *The computer will very probably revolutionize teaching — and learning — within a decade. It is already happening in its early stages.*
>
> *Computerized instruction can practically (and pleasurably) allow each student to learn more, faster, but always at his own pace. Individualized instruction, the ultimate dream of effective education, is well within the range of possibility. And, by spurring students to think experimentally, computers may eventually spark imaginative, independent thinking.*[9]

(The ad goes on to describe the great need for steel that these big mainframe computers and the air-conditioned rooms that housed them would require, and Republic Steel's readiness to supply it.) Who needs teachers when computers can teach students so efficiently?

Two decades later, in the late 1970s and early 80s, I entered this story of technological innovation in education as a high school history teacher. At the time, the newest wave of technological promise was the microcomputer. Powerful, relatively inexpensive, and increasingly accessible, the microcomputer was poised to distribute computing power into individual classrooms, offices, and homes. This technology was going to change my life as a teacher. At least, that's what the articles our department head handed out claimed. The microcomputer would relieve the drudgery of teaching, and, according to Seymour Papert of the Massachusetts Institute of Technology, it would do even more. In his influential book *Mindstorms,* Papert envisioned a future in which the computer might eliminate the need for schools altogether.

> *I believe that the computer presence will enable us to so modify the learning environment outside the classrooms that much if not all the knowledge schools presently try to teach with such pain and expense*

Most of the rhetoric about microcomputers depicted dramatic and wonderful change far beyond that delivered by earlier technological innovations.

and such limited success will be learned, as the child learns to talk, painlessly, successfully, and without organized instruction.[10]

No more organized instruction? That vision certainly would change my life. I guess I'd need to find a new job. Most of the rhetoric about microcomputers didn't go quite as far as Papert's, but it did depict dramatic and wonderful change far beyond that delivered by earlier technological innovations.

In the midst of such grand promise, our school determined to plunge ahead, and I was the one designated to lead the technology integration charge for our social studies department. Why was I selected? Well, I was the young one on the staff, which left me little choice in the matter. In addition, my housemate at the time was an economist who actually owned a personal computer, a Radio Shack Model III. That meant that, by proximity, I had more experience with the technology than anyone else in my group. I accepted the responsibility with the enthusiasm of a novice educational reformer. I had none of the historical perspective I've just summarized. I was simply excited about the possibility of change, having just cut my educational teeth on *The Open Classroom Reader* and MACOS (Man, A Course of Study). Reform was the name of the game, and, fresh from a progressive Yale education, I was ready to play.

With the help of my older brother and my housemate, I dove into the technology. My brother supported the effort by buying me my own computer — a $99 Timex Sinclair with a 16k RAM pack. This bargain computer was about the size of a desktop calculator. I had to use my television set as monitor and a cassette tape recorder as a storage device (what we now call a disk drive). With the help of my housemate I learned a bit of BASIC, which was one of the first simple computer programming languages. You see, the only way to get programs to use with my computer was to write them myself. It was a complicated process, but I had no family or other external obligations to distract me from this adventure. By late fall, with lots of assistance, I had written a grading program and was averaging my students' grades on the computer.

I felt great pride in my creation, and it helped ease one of the more cumbersome parts of my teaching duties (an experience which I will describe more fully later in the book). However, the real promise of the technology, at least according to all the rhetoric, wasn't about what it could do for me. The payoff was supposed to be what the computer could do for my students. This was demonstrated one day during an in-service in the library. A man wheeled a computer into the room and showed us the cutting edge in instructional technology for social studies. Here was an example of how the computer could take over instructing my students. I sat on the edge of my seat in anticipation. The software, which I think was called *States & Capitals,* worked something like this: an outline of a state, say New Jersey, would appear on the screen. The student had to correctly identify the name of the state and its capital before the timer ran out or New Jersey blew up. Well, maybe it wasn't exactly like that, but it was close.

To be honest, I recall being fairly excited. After all, I was responsible for teaching the states and capitals, and, believe it or not, my students weren't all that interested. Having them memorize Carson City, Nevada, and Jefferson City, Missouri, was a bit painful. Could the computer do it without organized instruction? I could certainly see my students getting excited about blowing up New Jersey. Wow, maybe this instructional technology could actually work!

A Glitch in the System

As I proceeded down the path of implementing the software in my classroom, my enthusiasm quickly dwindled. First, I had logistical problems. I had many students and not too many computers. How could I make sure each child had a chance to blow up New Jersey? Whether the computers were in the back of my classroom or down the hall in the lab, rotating students through the machines or down the corridor would require quite a bit of organizational rethinking. Somehow, I'd have to keep track of who used the computer and how much time each student spent using it. Plus, I'd have to figure out what the rest of the class would be doing while some students were off learning states and capitals.

While I wasn't categorically opposed to reorganizing my classroom, I found it tough to justify just so that students would have more fun while memorizing the states and capitals. I had many more important concepts, skills, and content to convey. I wanted students to learn about history, cultures, and government. I wanted them to develop an appreciation of the past and how it could provide insights into contemporary situations. And I worked hard to make all those things happen. A primary source unit I created prompted my students to discuss the concept of freedom while comparing Athens and Sparta in Ancient Greece. I worked with the language arts teachers, attempting to coordinate their literature readings with the periods of history I was teaching. I loved to innovate and rearrange but only if the results justified the effort. States and capitals just didn't measure up, even if it did make use of the school's expensive new computers.

My diminished enthusiasm turned toward frustration. Here I was earning barely $10,000 a year, and the school wanted to invest in a bunch of machines that were just going to make my life more complicated without delivering any significant benefits that I could see (at least at the time). Maybe the machines could teach students the states and capitals. But I couldn't imagine these devices ever taking my place as a discussion leader, classroom manager, personal coach, motivator, or lecturer. None of these technological wonders could judge how well a student contributed in class, wrote a paper, or built a pyramid. I suggested that the

None of these technological wonders could judge how well a student contributed in class, wrote a paper, or built a pyramid.

money might be better spent on my salary. As a hard-working teacher, I deserved higher pay. That may be so, came the reply, but the technology holds such promise. The computer would surely revolutionize teaching and learning. Maybe I was actually standing in the way of something truly important.

Confused and skeptical, I took a leave from teaching to enter the doctoral program at the Harvard Graduate School of Education. I needed some perspective, and like the good historian I was, I looked to the past for guidance. As I traced the histories of various educational technologies[11] a number of patterns emerged. One pattern was the repeated failure of technologies like motion pictures and television to effect large-scale change in schools. These technologies, which began with grand promises to revolutionize education and possibly even replace teachers, often ended up being used as an every-other-Friday treat for students. Another pattern was a tendency among critics of the school system, past and present, to point to these failures as evidence of the educational establishment's resistance to reform. Despite great ideas and breakthrough technologies, schools and the people within them just refuse to change.

When the Old Was New

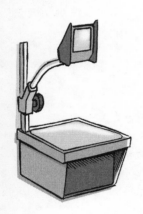

On the other hand, history also shows that schools have sometimes been quite willing to embrace new ideas and technologies. In the 19th century the dominant structure of schooling shifted from the one-room schoolhouse to age-graded classrooms, and a major shift in pedagogy followed. Over the decades educators willingly experimented with experiential education, classrooms without walls, constructivism, and much more. Teachers also welcomed many new technologies. The filmstrip, the overhead projector, the ditto machine, and the photocopier all achieved relatively high levels of integration into the regular school day. Even the chalkboard, a standard fixture in classrooms, was at one point a novel technology searching for a home in 19th-century common schools. Indeed, the history of the chalkboard offers several surprising insights.

Two separate stories describe individuals dazzled by chalkboard use in the early 1800s. In 1817, Professor Claude Crozet, a French officer, introduced this amazing device to the Academy at West Point. Crozet was assigned to teach engineering, but he found his pupils lacking the necessary background. He set out to instruct them in a relatively new science known as Descriptive Geometry, but he had no textbook, at least none in English. The story continues:

> *Geometry is not a thing to be taught orally. What is to be done? It was here at this precise time that Crozet, by aid of the carpenter and painter, introduced the blackboard and chalk. It is a very simple thing, and so is everything which is useful; but we know of no mere adjunct of teaching so useful as the blackboard.*

And the description of Crozet in action was inspiring. "We now see Crozet with his blackboard before him, chalk in hand, an animated, intellectual face, about to teach his class a new science, without a textbook."[12] This vivid description captured what many saw as the power of chalkboard technology.

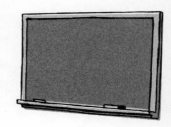

A similar recounting is found in the reminiscences of Reverend Samuel J. May. Looking back from the year 1866, May describes an even-earlier encounter with this classroom tool. In the following, May talks about a visit during his college vacation to a mathematical school in Boston, about 1813–1814:

> *On entering [the instructor's] room, we were struck at the appearance of an ample blackboard suspended on the wall, with lumps of chalk on a ledge below, and cloths hanging at either side. I had never heard of such a thing before. There it was — forty-two years ago — that I first saw what now I trust is considered indispensable in every school — the blackboard — and there that I first witnessed the processes of analytical and inductive teaching.*[13]

As word spread about this incredible device and the amazing learning experiences it helped to generate, reformers began scrambling to introduce the chalkboard into every common school classroom. The chalkboard seemed like such a natural fit, and it promised so much. By the early 1840s, almost every classroom in the northeastern U.S. had been outfitted with a chalkboard. Yet at first teachers failed to embrace the technology. Henry Barnard, one of the most notable educational reformers of the time, complained about lack of use in Connecticut schools. "Blackboards are not uncommon," he wrote in an annual report, "but are but little resorted to by the teacher."[14] The teacher had been handed an exciting new tool for education, and, according to William Alcott, another reformer of the time, he "knows almost as little how to use it as his pupils."[15] Alcott pointed not just to teacher ignorance about how to use the tool, he also accused teachers of an unwillingness to try. Can you imagine a teacher walking into a classroom, seeing a big chalkboard on the wall, giving it a bewildered look, and wondering, "How does it work?" Apparently 19th-century teachers found the chalkboard as daunting as many teachers today find the computer.

Apparently 19th-century teachers found the chalkboard as daunting as many teachers today find the computer.

The historical rhetoric about the chalkboard sounds a lot like the concerns voiced today about computers in education. We've put the machines in the classrooms, but the teachers aren't using them. The students know how to use them better than the teachers do. And the response has been similar: in-service training. In 1842, Alcott wrote his own how-to book called *Slate and Black Board Exercises for Common Schools,* and Josiah Bumstead included step-by-step instructions in *The Blackboard in the Primary School.*[16] Despite teachers' initial confusion, the chalkboard didn't take long to become a staple of classroom existence, not just for pioneering teachers but for everyone. Forty years after the chalkboard first entered common school classrooms, it had become well-established as an essential part of school architecture, a piece of educational technology that teachers demanded as part of their daily routine. Computers started pushing their way into schools in the 1960s, yet today advocates still call for more training and critics and academics wonder if the investment has been worth it.[17] Why the difference? Was it simply better in-service training for chalkboards than there has been for computers?

Why Technology Is Not That Easy

The answer, I suggest, becomes clear when we look at the differences between what I will call the programmed technologies — motion pictures, TV, and computers — and the dependent technologies, like the chalkboard. The proponents of the chalkboard, the overhead projector, the textbook, and even the filmstrip all assumed that the devices would work in concert with the teacher. Recall the descriptions of Crozet using his homemade blackboard and chalk, and what Reverend May witnessed. Both highlighted how the chalkboard elevated the energy and skill of the instructor. The value of the technology depended on how it worked in the hands of a teacher.

How surprised should we be that technologies designed to work independent of the teacher have struggled to find a regular home in the classroom?

How surprised should we be that technologies designed to work independent of the teacher have struggled to find a regular home in the classroom? These technologies lack the flexibility inherent in more useful classroom tools. Consider the differences between a film and a filmstrip, as educational reformers in the 1940s did when they sought to understand why educational film had failed so dismally to live up to its expectations. A 1946 article on new teaching materials in *The School Review* summarized the research of Mark May at Yale University. May stressed the need for teachers to integrate films as part of their broader "learning unit." However, the editors at the journal recognized the difficulty of molding films to fit the instructor's purpose. They noted, "Teachers who have found the motion picture a relatively formal means of presenting subject matter are turning more and more to the filmstrip, which adapts readily to the type of utilization suggested by May."[18] The filmstrip is a flexible technology. It is easy to start and stop, and invites the teacher to manage its use, elaborating on some frames while quickly skipping over others. A film, while much more visually stimulating, is inflexible. It is meant to be shown from start to finish. It's quite difficult to insinuate yourself into a film lesson, and it was especially difficult in the old days when stopping a film projector risked breaking or burning the film.

Access to the technology is another important difference between the technologies that were readily embraced by teachers, like the chalkboard, and those that were not, like film and computers. As a teacher in the pre-VCR era, I rarely had an opportunity to preview a film before I used it in my classroom. I didn't have a

16mm projector at home. If I wanted to preview a movie — to watch it carefully enough to figure out how to weave it into a coherent lesson — I needed to find time and access at school. That was no easy task. The school had a limited number of projectors, all housed in the library. If I wanted to use one, I had to sign up for it, and access was limited to the school day. Consequently, my film preview time was limited to my already crammed 42-minute preparation period. Even when I could find a free projector, I'd run out of time long before the movie was over. The result: I watched most movies for the first time in the classroom with my students. In other words, I did what Mark May complained teachers were doing back in 1946. I employed the "still too common method of 'showing' a film as an independent event rather that as an integrated part of the learning unit."[19]

Now, I never had a chalkboard or an overhead projector at home, but I didn't need them to plan my lessons. I could plan what to write on the chalkboard without practicing with the chalk ahead of time. And to use the overhead projector, all I needed was some pieces of acetate and some transparency pens. I either created the overheads myself or carried pre-produced materials home with me for review.

When I first entered the educational technology field, access was a tremendous issue. Schools had few computers and teachers had fewer. That situation continues to change. Computers are becoming a fixture in classrooms, and most classrooms are connected to the Internet.[20] Increasingly, teachers have personal computers at home, also connected to the Internet. If the software is portable — if it can be accessed both from the place of use and the place of preparation — it has a much greater chance of being integrated into the curricular agenda.

Weaving Technology Into the Classroom

Despite increased access, however, computers remain on the periphery of core classroom instruction because they have failed to clear that other hurdle to classroom technology — flexibility. All too often classroom computers are used in ways that are little better than just "showing" a film. Instead of being woven into the regular curriculum, the computer is used as an independent event. A student goes off into the corner where the computer is kept and spends some time blowing up adverbs with diphthong bombs or shooting improper fractions from the sky. The student is occupied for a while, and the teacher demonstrates that the computer is being used. Once that's out of the way, teacher and student can get on to the real tasks of teaching and learning.

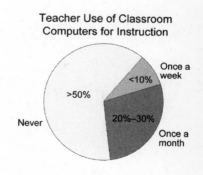

Teacher Use of Classroom Computers for Instruction

Larry Cuban, in his in-depth study of classroom computer use, *Oversold and Underused: Computers in the Classroom,* highlights the apparent contradiction of high access and low use. He found that: "Less than 10 percent of teachers who used computers in their classrooms were serious users (defined as using computers in class at least once a week); between 20 and 30 percent were occasional to rare users (once a month); well over half of the teachers were nonusers."[21] Teachers have the technology, but they still aren't using it. One reason they don't is that, like films, much software is designed to be used by students independent of the teacher. In fact, more than any previous technology, the public expectation is that computers are destined to take over the job of instruction.

One day, in the year 2000, at the height of the Internet frenzy that brought stock markets to unrealistically dizzying values, I sat next to a high-tech executive on a cross-country plane flight. We began to talk, and when I told him that I worked in educational technology, he quickly became very animated. He assumed that I was in the business of providing online education over the Web. He had a young child, and he expected that by the time she was ready for school, she would be doing most of her learning over the Internet. He explained that with all we've discovered about learning and the way the mind works, it must be simple for someone like me to design software that responds appropriately to a child's clicks in order to create a perfectly customized learning environment. The power of interactive technologies coupled with our expansive understanding of the brain should finally allow us to turn machines into perfect teachers.

I didn't know how to respond. Or maybe I just didn't know where to start responding. Like the well-meaning film advocates decades earlier, this intelligent individual assumed that the laws of the mind have been revealed — that we now have enough knowledge about how the brain works, coupled with enough computing power, to truly individualize instruction. His expectations, like the expectations of techno-enthusiasts before him, far exceed reality.

Certainly, we know more about the mechanics of learning and brain function than ever before, and we are gaining knowledge every day. We have new insights about language centers in the brain and the workings of memory. We can track how different stimuli activate different parts of the mind and speculate about what might be happening. It's exciting to see this research incorporated into educational practice, particularly in special education. But our questions still far outnumber our answers. Hindsight makes it easy for us to look back with a knowing sigh at the naïve assumption that films, following the laws of "habit" and "vividness," could teach the way teachers teach. Given that hindsight, can we say with certainty that computers can teach? Do we know enough to be able to accurately diagnose a student's current knowledge, skills, attitude, and needs, and then prescribe a tailored learning experience for that child that can meet our educational expectations?

We need to respect the incredible insights, intuition, and knowledge good teachers bring to the learning process already, and which no technology can replace. Rather than looking at how technology can replace teachers, maybe we should be looking at how technology and the new knowledge it enables can help teachers be better. The computer could fulfill its early promise to revolutionize education as a powerful administrative and instructional tool for teachers. But teachers won't begin to use this tool regularly until they find software and hardware that are designed to work in concert with them.

Because the computer is such a versatile tool, it presents many ways that it can be a teacher's partner and enhance the kind of teaching that leads to higher student performance and achievement. The computer can be like a chalkboard, a blank slate that the teacher uses to convey content and illuminate ideas. It can be like a film projector or VCR, animating and enriching important concepts. It can be a guide into a library of information for students to examine and peruse. It can be a manipulative environment for self-directed discovery. And it can also be a tireless coach, demanding the repeated exercise of fundamental skills. How and when it gets used in different ways for different purposes provides much of the focus for this book. In the chapters that follow I'll discuss how you can weave technology into the fabric of everyday teaching and learning, and give examples of specific software programs that will help you meet your educational goals. You'll discover ways that the computer can be your partner, inside the classroom and out, in the pursuit of educational success.

We need to respect the incredible insights, intuition, and knowledge good teachers bring to the learning process already, and which no technology can replace.

Using Technology Outside the Classroom

When I first started using a computer in school, I used it primarily as a gradebook.
I loved being able to instantly generate reports to give to students or to respond to
parent calls. Pretty soon I started using the computer to help with other tasks as well.
I can quickly make up worksheets, tests, or anything else I need, store it in the
machine and get to it whenever I want it.

It took a lot of time to get everything up and running — I had to find the software,
learn the programs, and design the systems I needed. But now, with everything working,
the computer has added at least two hours a day to my free time that I didn't have before.
Over four years, I've progressed from nowhere to everywhere.
It has made my life so much easier.

Mary Brown
6th-Grade Math Teacher
Francis Parker Middle School
San Diego, California

Using Technology Outside the Classroom

Let me start this section with a bold statement: Even if students never touch a computer in school, technology can have a powerful and positive impact on learning. Now, I'm not suggesting that students shouldn't use computers in school; an entire section of this book is devoted to that topic. But first, I want to raise awareness of the importance of teacher computer use. Over the last decade, the focus has been on increasing "access" — getting computers into schools and into the hands of students. Less emphasis has been placed on teachers as the primary users of computers, not just as instructional tools, but to help them perform all those regular before-and-after-school tasks that teachers perform. The success of what happens in the classroom when students are present relies heavily on what teachers do when the students aren't around. These tasks — grading student work, communicating with parents and other teachers, planning lessons — are critical components of the teaching and learning process.

When I was teaching, I was a "floater," moving from room to room for each class I taught. My desk in the high school social studies office was my only in-school workspace. It's the place where I spent my 42-minute preparation period each day. Forty-two minutes without students or cafeteria duty. Forty-two minutes to grade papers, prepare lessons, create ditto masters (yes, this was a long time ago), call parents, and attempt to preview that film I wanted to show later in the week. I just couldn't do it all. Forty-two minutes with interruptions from colleagues and students doesn't amount to much time. And as a novice teacher with little experience to draw from, I had a lot to prepare.

Unsurprisingly, my preparation time drifted into the afternoon. I would work diligently at my desk preparing lessons after the last bell rang and students headed home. But I soon found a number of my pupils staying after school to talk with me. Some wanted extra help. Some wanted to go beyond my curriculum. Some enticed me into supervising extracurricular activities. I couldn't refuse any of these requests, and as my day with students extended into the late afternoon, my preparation time was pushed into the evening. My real office became my dining-room table. I'd sit and read papers, average grades, review content, type worksheets, make critical phone calls to the parents of students on the edge of failure, devise lesson ideas, and so on. Sunday nights were especially frantic as I rushed to have a plan in place for the coming week. By my third year of teaching, as my confidence and experience grew, my sense of nightly panic eased a little bit, but my workday almost always dragged into a work night.

The success of what happens in the classroom when students are present relies heavily on what teachers do when the students aren't around.

Recently, I interviewed a group of teachers about their work life outside of the classroom. Things seem to have changed very little since my early teaching days. The results of my informal survey match the results of a much larger survey by the National Education Association. According to the NEA survey, teachers report spending an average of over eleven hours a week outside of the classroom doing things like grading papers and preparing lessons.[23] For new teachers, the weekly time commitment runs much higher, as it does for innovative teachers. But today, technology is an ingrained part of teachers' lives. According to *Education Week's* "Technology Counts" survey, "97 percent of all teachers surveyed use a computer at home and/or at school for professional activities."[24] For these teachers computer access, both at school and at home, has become a critical part of their preparation time. As they've discovered, technology can be a huge time-saver when you're performing all those critical outside-the-classroom tasks.

Communication

One important task that teachers perform when students aren't around is communication with everyone who isn't a student. Teachers do not work in isolation with their students, though some may occasionally wish they did. I know how I felt about communicating with other adults outside of my classroom. Oftentimes, I viewed these exchanges as intrusions. Worried questions from overprotective parents. Endless forms and requests from the administration. Faculty meetings during which many of my colleagues would sit in the back and grade homework. All of these duties and requests ate into my limited preparation time. Many teachers I talk to today voice similar feelings. They want the support of parents, administrators, and colleagues, and they want to contribute to success in other parts of the school, outside of their own classrooms. But they fear inviting more intrusions. Let's explore how technology can help you proactively manage your relationships with these individuals and groups to support your goals.

One important task that teachers perform when students aren't around is communication with everyone who isn't a student.

Communicating with Parents

Here's a typical conversation between me and my son about his school day:

> **Dad,** in a cheery voice: *Hey pal, how was school today?*
> **Son:** *Fine.*
> **Dad,** still cheery: *What did you do today?*
> **Son:** *Stuff.*
> **Dad,** sounding more interested and inquisitive: *Any special stuff?*
> **Son:** *Not really.*
> **Dad:** *Anything especially interesting?*
> **Son:** *Yeah.*
> **Dad,** on the edge of his seat: *What?*
> **Son:** *Stuff.*

You get the picture. Even well-meaning parents, like my wife and I try to be, can struggle to find out what's going on in their child's classroom if the main source of information is the child. Fortunately, from kindergarten through third grade we received a weekly newsletter from our son's teachers describing what went on in the classroom the previous week and what to expect in the coming week. We loved them! Armed with a bit of inside information, we could ask specific questions at dinner like, "Did you really dissect owl pellets?" or "Which Native American group are you going to research for the social studies project?" In fourth grade the newsletters became less frequent, and we missed them greatly. We felt disconnected from his life in the classroom. What book was the class reading? What science concepts and era of history were they studying? We had to go back to those painful conversations about "stuff."

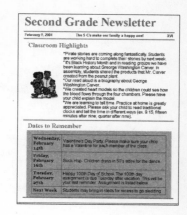

Now that you've heard my parent perspective on class newsletters, let me give my teacher perspective. When I taught, I never created a newsletter to go home to parents. In fact, I never created anything that would inform parents of what I was teaching their children. I was so busy planning for the next day, grading papers, and pulling together curriculum units, that communicating with parents never rose very high on my priority list. It was another thing to do, and I already had plenty of those.

Informed parents can be a teacher's best allies in the effort to raise student performance. According to research by Catherine Snow at the Harvard Graduate School of Education and others, parental talk about what young children are reading and doing builds rich vocabulary and enhances the child's ability to make connections. The impact is seen in literacy development and higher test scores.[25] As children get older, informed conversations about schoolwork can help validate the content you're teaching. If parents know what's being taught, they can ask specific questions and exhibit their own curiosity, reinforcing the interest you are trying to generate in the classroom.

Regular communication with parents can also reinforce a positive feeling about school for students. One of our son's teachers seemed to find a way to say something positive about each student in her class in each newsletter. It could have been something as simple as praising a student for following directions well or asking a good question. It didn't matter, because it gave us a reason to be proud and helped our son feel that school is a place where hard work can lead to success.

Informed parents can be a teacher's best allies in the effort to raise student performance.

Creating a Classroom News Web Page

As many teachers have discovered, technology makes it easy to create letters and newsletters to send home to parents. Most word processors and simple desktop publishing programs have a newsletter template that you can customize for your classroom. Whether or not you are currently using one of these programs to create newsletters, I'm going to assume that you're familiar with writing on a computer. Let's go beyond printed newsletters that are mailed out or sent home in students' backpacks, and jump right into fully electronic communication using e-mail and Web pages.

Now, I can hear what some of you out there are thinking. You can barely manage the time to create a print newsletter. Where are you going to find the time to learn how to make a Web page? Besides, if you already have a print version of a class newsletter going home in the backpack, why would you need an online version? Isn't the information already being sent out in a way that ensures universal access?

On the Web, important dates, colorful pictures from a field trip, shared accomplishments, and more can be retrieved at the click of a mouse.

The answer to the last question is yes and no. Yes, you are sending a print version home, but sending doesn't guarantee receipt. Students' backpacks are already bulging. Locating a relevant piece of paper from a child's backpack can seem to some parents like going on an archaeological dig. Old homework, new homework, doodles from the bus ride, half-completed projects, books, worksheets, clothes, and remnants of past lunches all compress in what for many students have become their portable lockers. Wouldn't it be nice for parents with Internet access to be able to read that information without having to dig for it? On the Web, important dates, colorful pictures from a field trip, shared accomplishments, and more can be retrieved at the click of a mouse.

Several companies offer online service that can help you create and post class newsletters and other Web pages. Scholastic's Class Homepage Builder provides the service for free with registration. Other companies, such as Tom Snyder Productions, McGraw-Hill Learning Network, and Education Planet, have a subscription service, usually with a low annual fee. With these online services, there's often no complicated software to install or programming language to learn. They usually have a tutorial that will guide you step-by-step to help you build and customize your pages online.

With the click of a button, the page is live on the Web. No need to track down your school's tech guru to upload it for you. In some cases, you don't even need to be at school to work on your Web page. If you have Internet access at home, you can create and upload your pages there. You may even be able to print out your Web page to distribute to families with no Internet access. Judy O'Dell, a 6th-grade teacher in Shreveport, Louisiana, says that increasing her communication with parents actually saved her time. "Last year, I began writing a weekly letter to parents that I posted on the Web. For the 10 parents who did not have Web access, I printed a copy and sent it home. I also posted daily homework assignments and a class calendar. I had fewer teacher conferences last year than ever before."

Creating an online classroom newsletter can help you keep parents informed. Visit these Web sites to learn more about how you can create and personalize your own Web page.

Scholastic's Class Homepage Builder
http://teacher.scholastic.com/ homepagebuilder/index.htm

Placemark (Tom Snyder Productions)
http://placemark.tomsnyder.com/ placemark

Education Planet's Teacher Web Tools
http://www.teacherwebtools.com

MySchoolOnline
http://www.myschoolonline.com

McGraw-Hill Learning Network
http://mhln.com

Quia.com Class Pages
http://www.quia.com

Scholastic's Class Homepage Builder *is free and easy to use.*

With Tom Snyder Productions' Placemark, *you can create a Web page and a printed newsletter at once.*

Teacher Tip

We use the Internet to facilitate parent and community involvement with our school — one of our School Improvement goals. Using *Placemark*, we created an online newsletter that keeps parents up to date with lunch menus, upcoming events, school/county issues, and teacher information such as welcome letters, supply lists, and field trips. The newsletter is also an excellent vehicle for showcasing students' work. We have had essay contests for the students to promote writing (another School Improvement goal). The winners earned an ice-cream treat and certificate, and their essays were published on our Web site in the next issue of the newsletter for all to share.

Joanus Harper
Pre-K–5 teacher
Osteen Elementary School
Osteen, Florida

Communicating Through E-mail

Web pages provide great broadcast vehicles for everything from class news to schedules to homework. E-mail presents another valuable way to communicate with parents who have Internet access that complements the broadcast feature of posted Web pages. As both a parent and a former teacher, I know how cumbersome it can be for parents and teachers to try to communicate. Most teachers are too busy during the school day to take phone calls. At my school, I picked up my messages at the end of the day from the main office. The game of telephone tag would then continue in the evening when I finally had a moment to return calls. As a parent, I've found myself using my son as a postal service. A note from us goes into his backpack. The teacher receives it (we hope!) and sends a reply the same way.

How much easier it's been when the teacher has an e-mail address that she checks regularly. We can clarify homework assignments, make arrangements for anticipated absences, coordinate volunteer efforts, and so on. My wife and I don't have to hope to catch our son's teacher at a mutually convenient time; we can converse at each other's convenience. As teacher Mary Brown at the Francis Parker Middle School in San Diego says, "Teachers are tired at the end of the day. They don't want to make a lot of phone calls. A phone conversation about a problem with a student can take 20–30 minutes. With e-mail, you just need a statement or two. I probably spend 5–10 minutes each day answering six or seven e-mails from parents. I e-mail parents if a child's homework is missing, or if I need something from them. They e-mail me if a child is sick or has a dentist appointment. The correspondence between home and school has improved so much, and it's been painless. I would say that e-mail is one of the best things the computer has done for teachers."

What about the parents who complain about everything, who want special treatment for their child, who want to revise your curriculum, and who think your reading list is too risqué? When you're interrupted at dinner by these types of telephone calls, it might be hard to keep the conversation calm and rational. With e-mail, you can deal with parent requests on your own time. You can think about and revise your responses before sending them. You can include administrators, guidance counselors, and other teachers in the conversation. And finally, if you ever did get bombarded by an abusive parent, the e-mail would give you a complete record of the time, date, and content of each message. For the most part, though, if you set a tone of open communication with parents, the positives will far outweigh the negatives. If you reach out to them, you'll find a large number of parents enlisted on your side, working with you to help you succeed with their children.

There are several free e-mail services on the Internet, such as **Yahoo! Mail** (http://mail.yahoo.com) and **Hotmail** (http://www.hotmail.com). However, if you're looking for a free AND safe e-mail service for your whole class, consider **Gaggle.net** (http://gaggle.net). You can set up a master account for yourself and a separate account for each of your students. As holder of the master account, you can review students' incoming and outgoing e-mails. Gaggle has a built-in monitoring system that blocks spam mail, curse words, and more. You can also customize the monitoring system according to your own preferences.

Communicating with Administrators and Colleagues

One of my first formal teaching experiences came in 1978 in the New Haven, Connecticut, public schools. As a practice teacher in one of the local high schools, I was given two courses in U.S. History and one in World Cultures to teach on my own. In this sink-or-swim trial by fire I had no set curriculum to follow. I didn't know what the students had previously learned. I didn't know what other teachers of the same classes were doing. I didn't know what next year's teachers were expecting from these students. And I had no personal experience to draw on. With support from two veterans at the school and my mentor at Yale, I learned and grew rapidly, and I wouldn't trade the experience for a more coddled apprenticeship. However, the experience did instill in me a sense of isolation as a classroom teacher. When I closed the door to my classroom, nothing else existed. The school administration intervened in the classroom only in the face of discipline or severe academic jeopardy. Opportunities for faculty members to meet, share, and work together were few and far between.

A few years later, as a certified, full-time teacher, I struggled to break out of the isolation of my classroom box. I wanted to coordinate my ancient and medieval history curriculum with relevant literature being taught in language arts. Lack of time, schedule conflicts, and limited resources made the effort futile. We just couldn't pull it off. It was a shame to lose an opportunity to reinforce related learning across content domains.

Teachers need to be part of a learning community, not stuck alone in their classrooms.

Today, as a member of my town's school committee (known as a school board in some parts of the country), I recognize the problems that teacher isolation can cause, not just for individual teachers, but within the school system. Droves of senior teachers are perched on the edge of retirement while schools bulge with the children of baby-boomers. According to one study, over 40% of new teachers don't expect to make teaching a lifelong career.[26] As we face a teacher shortage crisis, researchers have examined what it will take to keep teachers in the classroom. Mentoring for novice teachers, better support and professional development opportunities, and improved working conditions could help improve retention. Teachers need to be part of a learning community, not stuck alone in their classrooms.

In a learning community, teachers can not only benefit from each other's experiences, but they can build on learning from one grade to the next in a coordinated and thoughtful way. In the early school years, for example, as students learn to read and write, a coordinated approach from first grade to second grade to third grade isn't just nice, it's essential. In the handoff of students from one specialist to another and from one grade level to another, it can be easy to fumble the ball if we haven't coordinated the exchange. And a well-run play, not to overuse the football metaphor, has a much better chance for a long-gain than one that is haphazardly put together. Students benefit from good horizontal (within grade level and department teams) and vertical (across grade levels) communication.

Unfortunately, the same obstacles that stood in the way of my attempts to bring history and language arts together twenty years ago remain in place today. Time is short while demands are high. When can teachers, curriculum coordinators, and administrators actually sit down to talk and organize and plan, let alone implement a well-coordinated interdisciplinary curriculum?

Here's where technology, as a fantastic information disseminator, can make a difference. As I've already discussed, e-mail is a wonderful tool for carrying on conversations when demanding schedules prevent face-to-face meetings. Lisa DiSanzo, a special-education teacher at Watertown Middle School in Massachusetts says teachers at her school have grown to love the convenience of e-mail. "It's so much easier than picking up the phone and interrupting class, or running all the way to the office to write a note to stick in somebody's box. With e-mail, communication is quick and efficient." While e-mail correspondence can't take the place of a live dialogue, it can be used to ask questions, present ideas, and share information about individual students. And it can certainly act as a vehicle to let others know what you're planning to teach, when, and how. Every little bit of communication helps strengthen your learning community.

The Web can also be a vehicle for communicating with colleagues and for disseminating best practices within a school or district. District curriculum guides posted on the Web can serve as constant reminders of curriculum objectives that can't get lost, deleted, or buried under a stack of student work. Curriculum materials that teachers have created in digital form are simple to edit and refine, and can be easily shared over the Web. Tom Plati, Director of Libraries and Educational Technologies for the Wellesley Public Schools in Massachusetts, emphasizes the "home-grown curriculum" capabilities of *Placemark,* one of the Web page-building tools described earlier. In addition to using *Placemark* as a tool for parent communication, his teachers use it to create, share, and grow quality curriculum activities that meet local standards. For example, one of the 5th-grade teachers in the district used *Placemark* to develop and post a research project on Ancient Egypt.

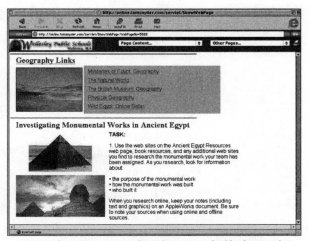

An Ancient Egypt research project created with Placemark

This pioneering teacher has researched useful and appropriate sites where students can gather information. She's created the tasks and schedule to complete the project. And it's a perfect fit for the district's 5th-grade curriculum. With the click of a button, she can share this lesson with all of her 5th-grade colleagues. In fact, the other 5th-grade teachers can open a copy of her Web page and edit the due dates, update and add Web links, modify the tasks to better fit their particular students, and repost it on the Internet for their own classes. It's instant quality curriculum sharing. By making this kind of sharing easier, technology can help pave the way for good efforts to spread throughout a school and district, bringing teachers out of their classroom shells and into a true community of committed educators.

Managing Grades and Student Information

I mentioned earlier that I launched my educational technology career with a grading program I created during my first years of teaching. Why did I build something as mundane as a grading program? The answer is pretty simple. I didn't have the skills to do anything complex, like a simulation. Plus, a grading program really helped me. As a high school social studies and history teacher, I carried as many as 150 students a semester in three different preparations. For each of those students, I attempted to keep track of homework assignments, quizzes, in-class participation, projects, reports, and tests, not to mention attendance and discipline. I struggled to fit all that information into the tiny boxes of the green gradebook I was handed at the beginning of each school year. At the end of each marking period I would sit with my gradebook and a calculator to figure each student's grade. Let's see. Homework was worth 20%, projects and reports 20%, and so on.

Once I started using a grading program I could calculate a student's average at the click of a button. As the task became less daunting, I could do it more often, much to the benefit of my students.

Averaging grades was a big project, so I didn't do it very often. Although I tried to have a sense of how each of my students was doing, inevitably at the end of the semester I'd find one or two quiet students who somehow had gradually stopped working midway through the marking period. Waiting until the end of a marking period to figure out grades didn't give students a lot of time to change their habits and attitudes to affect their report cards. If I had uncovered the problem earlier, I might have been able to take action at a more opportune moment. Once I started using a grading program, though, I could calculate a student's average at the click of a button. As the task became less daunting, I could do it more often, much to the benefit of my students.

Student	Average	1	2	3	4	5	6	7	8	9	10
Boone, Melissa	96.8	96	102	103	84	96	92	100	100	95	100
Bosco, Beth	89.0	96	100	91	96	88	78	88	90	75	88
Bukjiok, Tang	80.2	84	95	84	76	72	68	80	75	80	88
Callinan, Jeremy	83.0	96	85	94	79	80	70	84	95	75	72
Chaney, Mike	98.7	100	102	103	95	104	96	100	95	100	92
Chang, Tai Li	87.3	92	95	91	72	92	96	84	85	90	76
Coric, Omer	89.6	76	95	94	93	72	96	96	80	100	84
Cubulskis, David	81.4	96	100	67	67	92	76	84	90	70	72
Debartolo, Jay	95.9	92	102	91	96	96	92	100	100	90	100
Fuller, Kym	97.2	96	90	103	96	96	96	100	100	95	100
Galaska, Dave	90.0	92	95	88	96	84	84	96	90	85	90
Galata, Brad	86.0									80	92
Junkins, Nisco	89.0	88	102	100	87	88	100	72	85	100	68
Kidder, Haley	92.5	96	105	97	92	96	96	84	95	80	84
Mirras, Dave	86.0	84	95	88	68	64	88	84	95	90	96
Navarro, Ben	89.6	92	95	94	92	72	96	84	85	90	96
Pacai, CM	89.5	92	100	73	91	96	92	80	85	90	96
Shukis, Billy	86.4	96	100	76	91	96	80	80	75	70	100

A customized spreadsheet gradebook made with Excel

Having gradebook software helped in other ways, too. One simple example is the relative ease of finding mistakes in an electronic system. It wouldn't be unusual for me to plug grades into a calculator and look dumbfounded at the result. The final average just didn't look right for that student. Had I missed an assignment from my book? Had I transposed a number? Or did the student actually perform worse than I'd expected? Maybe I just couldn't read my own writing. I had to recalculate from scratch. On the other hand, I always knew with my computerized gradebook that there could be no calculation mistake. I just had to recheck the grades I'd entered. Oops! I'd typed in a 19 instead of a 99 for a major test for this student.

Back in 1981, if you wanted a computerized grading program, you had to sit down, learn a programming language, and write one for yourself. Today, it's a lot easier. Teachers are building their own customized gradebooks with simple spreadsheet programs like *AppleWorks* or Microsoft *Excel.* In fact, the educational versions of these programs typically include spreadsheet templates that make it relatively easy to create a custom gradebook.

There are also many commercial gradebook packages on the market today. Preview a gradebook program if you can, and play around with it for a while. You'll discover options that make what you already do easier, and some options that you never thought were possible. Some gradebook programs even let you import student pictures to create seating charts, useful at the beginning of the year when you're just learning students' names, or if a substitute teacher is taking your class for a day or two. As you evaluate gradebook software, keep in mind that the outputs, print or electronic, should mesh with your school's system for distributing report cards to students. You don't have to retype all that information — let the technology do the work for you.

Some schools have even gone a step further, purchasing school-wide systems that track not only grades, but attendance, standardized test scores, and demographic information. When all of this data flows into one school or district-wide student information management system, student, teacher, and school performance can

············

Creating a Gradebook with Excel

Excel *is a powerful program that you can use to create your own customized spreadsheet gradebook.*

▶ *Turn to page 104 for step-by-step instructions on creating a gradebook, reprinted from the book* Excel Workshop for Teachers *by Janet Caughlin.*

Some popular gradebook programs: GradeQuick, mygradebook.com, and Class Action Gradebook.

Teacher Tip

I use *Excel* to record grades in reading, math, and spelling. I appreciate the ease with which I can manipulate data. I like formatting all grades below 80 in red. It is easy to see if a certain concept was difficult for all, or if some child is frequently falling below the 80 mastery level. The formatting capabilities allow me to make my gradebook easy to read and understand. The chart-making capabilities of *Excel* are fantastic. It is so easy to create attractive, understandable charts. Parents really seem to appreciate the charts.

Carolyn Nordstrom
1st-grade teacher
Clarkson Elementary School
Fremont, Nebraska

Design your own gradebook using spreadsheet software, or choose from any of these commercial gradebooks:

- **GradeQuick**
  (Jackson Software)

- **Class Action Gradebook**
  (CalEd Software)

- **Grade 2 Second Generation Electronic Gradebook**
  (Excelsior Software, Inc.)

- **ClassMaster** (William K. Bradford Publishing Company)

- **A2Z Gradebook** (A2ZWare)

- **FastTracker GradeBook**
  (Calico Software Inc.)

You can also create your own gradebook on the Web:

- **MyGradeBook**
  http://www.mygradebook.com

be evaluated in new and interesting ways. Just as an individual gradebook can allow you to get printouts, averages, distributions, and specific records on any student or class at any time, an integrated school-wide system extends this power to school administrators. Some of these systems even allow parents ongoing access to their children's performance records, attendance, discipline issues, and more.

Whether you choose to create your own spreadsheet gradebook, invest in a commercial program, or log in to a full-blown student information management system, you can reap worthwhile results. By making it easier to let students know when their grades are dipping or assignments are missing, you can spark your pupils into action and improve student performance. One teacher from New Jersey, Dana Freeman, had this to say about a piece of grading software he had discovered.

The most important result of using this program is that my students appear to be taking a more active and responsible role in their own education. As soon as I begin to detect a pattern, I pull the student aside with the strong suggestion that the situation be corrected soon — before I have to contact the home. But, more and more...I find that students are having to be talked to less and less about those missing assignments. Does this mean that I'm seeking to shun some of my duties? No, actually the program has allowed me to spend more of my time TEACHING!

Grades are just part of the information you want to maintain about your students. In addition to my gradebook, I used to keep an index card for each student, containing the student's name, parents' names, phone numbers, and so on. My intention was to write down on the card the date and content of each call home and each meeting with the student. Well, despite my best intentions, my card system never lasted that long. It was just too cumbersome to carry from class to class and from home to school. Plus I had a tough time finding the right card when I needed it. For instance, I'd write a note on a student's card and then weeks later forget which student's record I had updated. Keeping the cards alphabetized was a pain in the neck, and of course I was always running out of room.

The system itself wasn't entirely at fault; I had some flaws too, including poor handwriting and less-than-stellar organizational skills. I often had trouble reading my notes, and I had a habit of putting index cards down amidst piles of paper and losing them. To work well, the index-card system required lots of maintenance and organization, and even then it was limited.

Thankfully, computers are much more capable of organizing and keeping track of this information than I was. With a searchable database, I don't have to worry about losing track of information I collect. After each conversation with a student or phone call home I make a note in the database. I can even copy important e-mail messages and include them in the database. Then when I want to look something or someone up, I just search by keyword. Or I can sort the records in order of the last date they were edited to help me find that note I wrote last week about some-one (when I can't remember who that someone is). And I never have to worry about messy handwriting or running out of space. Setting up a student database is not difficult, and most database utilities, like the one in *AppleWorks*, have a template to get you started.

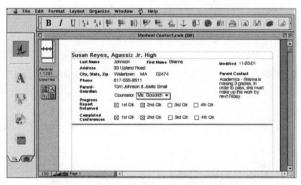

Keep track of student information with an AppleWorks *database.*

Putting student information in the computer does have some limitations. One limitation is portability. A card system is easier to carry around than my desktop computer. And I never had to wait for my index cards to "boot up" to jot down a quick note. Of course if you have a computer and Internet access at home as well as at school, you could use an online system to access the information in all the places you work. With the development of personal digital assistants, it likely won't be long before portability is no longer an issue. You've just got to look at your life and see what's right for you before you start making everything electronic.

••••••••••

Creating a Student Address Database with AppleWorks
You can use a database to record and organize all kinds of information about students, from names and addresses to grades to anecdotal records. With a database you can easily search your records, print reports, and even create a mail merge to easily address letters you're mailing home.

▶ *Turn to page 110 for step-by-step instructions on creating a name and address database with AppleWorks, reprinted from the book* AppleWorkshop for Teachers *by Janet Caughlin.*

Lesson Planning

One of the most essential and creative tasks teachers face almost every day is figuring out how to teach the curriculum. While most of what I had to teach was dictated by a combination of local, state, and national frameworks and tests, how I taught that content was up to me. I loved the challenge. How could I get students excited about the Peloponnesian Wars? How could I make sure they would remember the hierarchies of medieval life? How could I plant in them the seeds of a lifelong love for history?

During my first few years teaching I was overwhelmed with learning what I had to teach. Having taken one undergraduate course in the history of Ancient Greece, I found myself teaching a year of ancient and medieval history, from prehistory through the 16th century, along with two other preparations. I spent many nights reading, trying to stay a bit ahead of my students. I had retained rights to visit the library at Yale, and I used it as a resource to help piece together a packet of primary source materials about freedom in Athens and Sparta, as well as a packet of materials on the role of the Church during the Middle Ages.

Today, technology puts a vast array of information and resources into the hands of teachers and students.

Today, technology puts a vast array of information and resources into the hands of teachers and students. The information on medieval art and architecture that I spent hours digging out of the library stacks is now compiled in CD-ROM databases. Try logging onto the Internet and typing "Medieval primary sources" into a search engine. When I did it, the result was a list of nearly 2,000 sites, including some that contained interesting primary source text and one that had a great summary of what primary sources are and how to use them. How long would it have taken me to find similar useful information in the library stacks?

On the other hand, the limited materials available at the library were much more manageable than the 2,000 sites I found on the Internet. Who has time to check the information from all those sources? It can be overwhelming. Where did the facts come from? Are they accurate? Sometimes the Internet feels like a bad smorgasbord: An incredible amount of food is laid out for you, but most of it doesn't taste very good. On the Internet, anyone can become a publisher. It is fairly easy and inexpensive for me to publish pictures of my wedding, my son's birthday party, and our last family vacation. At the same time I could easily publish and distribute propaganda, misinformation, and pornography. Traditional print publishers provide an important service to busy people. They filter and validate the content that they publish. The Internet leaves that process in your hands, and it takes a lot of time, knowledge, and often a healthy dose of skepticism.

These problems don't mean that the Internet isn't a valuable resource. You just have to be smart about how you use the enormous amount of information it makes available. You can solve the validity issue by sticking with sites you know and trust. Government organizations such as the Smithsonian Institution, the Library of Congress, and the CIA all have valuable data available on the Internet. Museums and universities are also reliable sources to consider. And print publishers that you trust may have made some of their resources available online. The Internet also gives you a mechanism for searching for traditional print materials right from your desk, since many libraries' catalogs are now online. Over time you'll discover good sites with reliable resources that support your lesson development.

In addition to helping you gather information for your lessons, the Web can also connect you to colleagues for an exchange of ideas. Type "lesson plans" into an Internet search engine and you'll find many sources of ideas to bring into your classroom. Type in "teacher discussion board" and you'll find networks of teachers with whom you can share thoughts, techniques, and lesson plans via live chat sessions or e-mail. But as with other online information, the best strategy may be to start with sources that you know and trust. Your colleagues or curriculum coordinators, for instance, may be developing lessons that exactly match your curriculum and needs. Taking advantage of their efforts through the school's local computer network or through an online service saves you the time of sifting through thousands of possibilities to find the ones that are right for you.

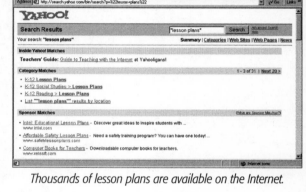

Thousands of lesson plans are available on the Internet.

Finally, as you plan your lessons, the computer can help you organize your ideas. When I sat down to prepare a lesson or series of lessons, I would gather all the information I had collected for the unit (usually quite a lot). Then I'd make a list of the specific content and skills that I wanted students to acquire. Now, in what order should the information be presented? What wonderful anecdotes go with which point? What information should be presented by me and what uncovered through directed discovery? As I answered these questions, I would create a structure, or set of structures, that divided the whole unit into bite-sized lessons.

I now use an organizing program called *Inspiration,* published by Inspiration Software, to help me create such structures and outlines on the fly. Imagine you're sitting at your computer, surrounded by books, papers, and notes. You reach for each piece of information and enter it, or a summary of it, into the computer. With *Inspiration* you can throw your data onto the screen with little order at all. At some point in the process, you can begin to connect the pieces, to give them some order and organization. You attach anecdotes to concepts and skills to activities. You rearrange and reorganize. Make a few more connections and switch to the outline view. When you're done you will have two organizational structures to help you pull together your information. You will also have two

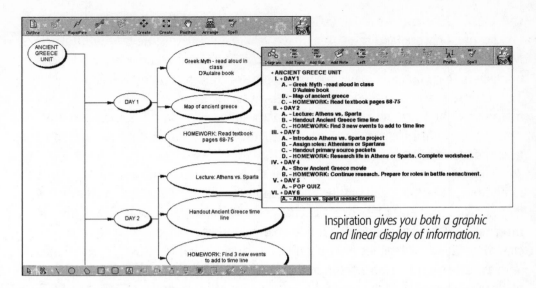

*Inspiration gives you both a graphic
and linear display of information.*

views to share with your students — one highly graphic, the other more linear (both shown here). If you wanted to change your connections for another class, you would merely reorganize. Once it's in the computer, you don't have to recreate your lesson from scratch every time you want to make a change. With a dynamic tool like *Inspiration,* it becomes easy to create better-organized lessons and some nice printouts and displays for your students.

Creating Classroom Materials

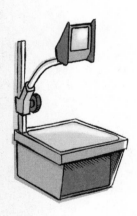

If you can use the computer to create letters and newsletters for parents, you can also use it to create worksheets, handouts, and quizzes for students. In fact, making information look good has been one of the most consistent promises of the computer. As far back as December, 1987, Apple Computer ran an ad in *The Wall Street Journal* that carried this very message. The three-page spread opened with a large picture of a device familiar to the worlds of both education and business: an overhead projector. In the upper right-hand corner of the page was the following message: "WARNING: Improper operation of this machine may cause headaches, nausea and drowsiness."

I could identify with that image, and the text elaborated. Apple, the ad proclaimed, was here "to save humanity (and you) from the deadliest of sins: Boring people in public." No more "brain-numbing overheads, eye-glazing slides, and soul-deadening presentation handouts." Although the ad was describing a typical business meeting, my mind conjured up a vision of an all-too-typical classroom. As a student and as a teacher, I knew that I had been both bored and boring. My students were none too shy about announcing, sometimes in rather unpleasant ways, when their attention had begun to drift from the lesson at hand. The promise that I could easily create "dazzling, scintillating, graphically compelling overheads,

35mm color slides, and leave-behinds that don't get left behind" was very compelling. It still is. Succeeding in the "Information Age" requires more than just gathering and analyzing information. You also have to present it. Presenting information is something teachers do a lot, and the computer can help.

At the most basic level, a computer can help you simply keep your handouts up to date, even if it doesn't help them look much better. The ability to edit, which even beginning computer users now take for granted, can help improve the quality of teaching. Certainly the time saved on retyping materials can be better spent on parent communication and lesson planning. Of course, word processors now have some of the features of more complicated desktop publishing programs. Not only can you edit your work, you can organize it on a page so that it is easier to read and understand. You can paste in graphics, change font size, and print in color. You can make transparencies for your overhead projector. With a simple word processor, you can do what Apple promised over a decade ago.

And with more than a word processor, you can do…well, more. Specific software programs can help you create all kinds of interesting and valuable materials for your classroom. Some of these programs are straightforward quiz- and test-making programs. Others offer more interesting and unusual opportunities. Whether you're making worksheets and quizzes, graphs, maps, or even awards for your students, there are specific software programs that can help.

Worksheets

There was a time when, as a good progressive educator, I thought that "worksheets" represented all that was wrong with traditional, teacher-centered education. Worksheets, I believed, were boring and repetitive. They squelched student creativity and ownership of their learning. I looked down at them with disdain, and I know many educators who shared that view. Then, I became a parent and looked at learning from a new perspective. My son, for instance, needed to practice his computational skills. A worksheet full of computation problems provided a very efficient means for that practice. He needed to learn the multiplication table so well that it became automatic. Flashcards did a pretty good job supporting that effort. He needed to write a reading response each week. A graphic organizer worksheet gave him an excellent supporting structure for organizing his ideas.

Worksheets, it turns out, can be alright. From coloring in a map to help learn U.S. geography to solving a crossword puzzle to reinforce vocabulary, completing a worksheet can help support targeted curriculum goals quite well. How many have you created over the years for your students — crossword puzzles, hidden-word games, connect the dots, mazes, blank maps, hangman, and so on? Some of these worksheets you may have photocopied from a book of helpful activities.

Others you may have created yourself. Check out an educational software catalog under the category of "Teacher Utilities" or "Productivity Tools." You'll find several applications, many written by current or former teachers, that make creating fun worksheets very easy to do. Tom Snyder Productions publishes a series of CD-ROMs called *Essential Tools for Teachers*. (Some of these programs are also available as an Internet subscription.) With these tools you can easily create all kinds of handouts including worksheets, puzzles, and quizzes. Other similar products include *Zybura's Toolbox for Teachers* (Zarb), *Hot Potatoes* (Half-Baked Software), and *WISCO Word Power* (WISCO Computing). You may also want to explore Discovery School's Teaching Tools online at http://school.discovery.com/teachingtools/teachingtools.html.

Math, Word, and Vocabulary Worksheets

Not only have many of the worksheets my son has brought home helped him, he even enjoys them. As one elementary teacher once whispered to me, "Kids like 'em." There is something satisfying about completing an appropriately challenging set of narrow tasks. The key here is "appropriately challenging." Not all students master the same skill set at the same time. Ideally, you want to create targeted worksheets that represent the range of skills among your students — a math worksheet filled with multiplication of two- and three-digit numbers for some students and one with multiplying decimals for others; a spelling worksheet with added "challenge" words for some kids but not for everyone. One of the great balancing acts that teachers perform is keeping each student engaged at the right level, particularly in elementary school as fundamental skills are evolving at different rates. The *Essential Worksheets* programs let you pick the specific skills you want to cover for your whole class or for a selected group of students, and then generate the worksheet.

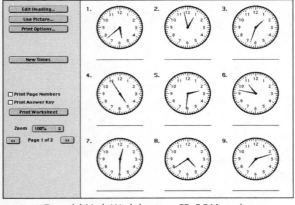

Essential Math Worksheets – *CD-ROM version*

Fun Puzzles and Stuff

In addition to the straightforward practice presented by the worksheets described above, students can also hone their skills with crossword puzzles, word searches, and other fun activities. With some of the programs mentioned above, you can create them, along with mazes, math quotes, cross sums, and more with ease. Just type in the words and clues or select the objectives you want to cover, and the computer does the rest. The software will create and lay out the puzzle for you. If you don't like the way the software has organized the puzzle, you can usually click a button to rearrange it. Then all you need to do is print and photocopy the puzzle.

Essential Puzzles – *CD-ROM version*

Quizzes and Tests

Students hate them. I was never a big fan either. But tests seem to be a bigger part of our lives than ever before. Almost every state in the nation has a set of curriculum standards, along with tests to measure student performance on those standards. These tests tend to include two formats: multiple choice and essay (either short or long). Students are asked to interpret reading passages, graphs, and images. Students must demonstrate their ability to recall information, use specific skills, and apply concepts. As measuring sticks for how students are progressing toward mastering the curriculum standards, classroom tests and quizzes can play a role. You can use software like the *Essential Tools* programs to help you format test content that you create. You write the questions, select the graphics, and indicate the question type (multiple choice, fill in the blank, essay, etc.). The software creates the test in the appropriate format, ready to be printed and reproduced. Over the years, you can build up a pool of questions that you can use to instantaneously generate tests.

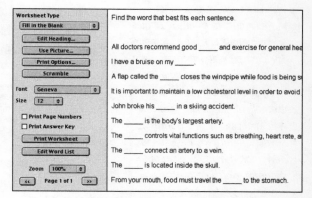

Essential Word Worksheets – *CD-ROM version*

Time Lines

One common classroom sight, especially in social studies classes, is a time line — a long banner stretched around the room displaying the order of historical events. Time lines serve a very useful purpose as a quick reminder of cause-and-effect relationships and the relative passage of time. But time lines can be difficult to create. It's not so much putting the events in order that's hard, it's figuring out the proportional spacing, especially when your time line stretches across many pieces of paper or is on a long roll of paper. It can take a lot of measuring. And then adding or deleting an event means everything has to be remeasured to keep the proportional spacing between events correct. By hand, it's a pain. On the computer, with a program such as *TimeLiner*, it's a breeze.

TimeLiner, by Tom Snyder Productions, is simple and straightforward. It makes time lines — a day long, a week long, a year long, or many years long. You enter the events in any order you like, and the program arranges them chronologically, spaces them proportionally, and can give you a nice big banner- or poster-size printout. *TimeLiner* allows you and students to focus on the content of your time line rather than getting bogged down in the mechanics of calculating the distance between each event. And it allows you to merge two time lines with ease.

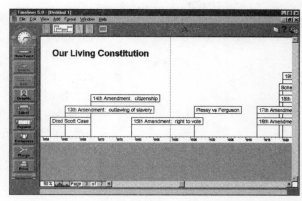

TimeLiner *makes it easy to create time lines for your classroom.*

Creating a School Year Time Line with TimeLiner

TimeLiner is a program that makes it easy to create, illustrate, and print time lines. Turn to page 119 for step-by-step instructions for creating a school-year time line. You'll also find a reproducible example of a time line created with TimeLiner. Visit the Tom Snyder Productions Web site to download a demo version of the program, watch an overview movie, and even get ready-made time lines to use with the program.
www.tomsnyder.com/weaving

TimeLiner can be used to illustrate relative values other than time.

Illustrative Time Lines

Time lines are often used in history to help students understand sequences of events and various cause-and-effect relationships. Time lines, though, are also very helpful in literature. Books and stories are not always presented in sequential order. Plotting time lines can help students better comprehend what they read. In addition, the proportional spacing feature of *TimeLiner* can be used to illustrate relative values other than time. Laurie Olafson, a teacher in Washington, uses *TimeLiner* to show students the relative distances of planets from the sun in our solar system. She says,

> *First, I put the planets on the time line, using 0 for the sun, and putting in the miles from the sun without the zeros. Mercury was 36, Venus 67, Earth 93, Mars 142, Jupiter 483, Saturn 887, Uranus 1783, Neptune 2794, Pluto 3666. The printout really shows the relationship of the planets and how far Pluto really is from Earth. Second, I put in the planet diameters, and then put butcher paper drawings of the planets next to the time line, with the smaller planets on top of the larger ones.*

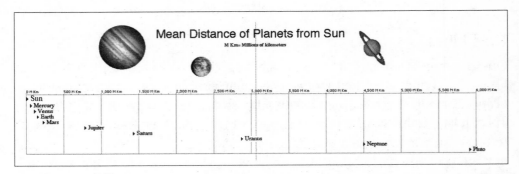

Other time lines showing relative size might include the height of students in a class, number of calories in food, or mileage run by the track team. With *TimeLiner* you can set whatever scale you desire. I've tried some of these suggestions. They're fun, and they work.

Organizational Time Lines

"I didn't know that was due today." "I thought we had another week for this project." Getting students, or almost anyone for that matter, to meet deadlines is a tough task. *TimeLiner* makes it easy to generate both short- and long-term schedules that can be posted for everyone to see. A teacher in New York made a giant time line of his curriculum and tacked it up around the room. Everyone knew what was coming and when. Of course, it wasn't long before they were off schedule. It's a good thing the program is easy to edit. A 6th-grade class in Wyoming had a more creative scheduling idea. The kids had a tough time remembering the deadlines for the annual science fair. With the help of *TimeLiner* and Dr. I. M. Madd, a wild cutout character, they made their due dates. Dr. Madd was constructed with outstretched hands in which he held first monthly time lines and then daily ones that displayed the schedule for the approaching fair. According to the teacher, "the students not only remembered the deadlines but had fun reading about them."

Graphs

Graphs are part of the math curriculum from the earliest grades. Students must analyze and interpret graphs on standardized tests. They encounter them every day in the newspaper and in advertisements. Since graphs are so important, it makes sense for teachers to include them on worksheets and wall charts. Computers, with the right kind of software, make the creation of these graphs not only easy, but fun too.

If you have *AppleWorks* or Microsoft *Excel,* you have the capability to create graphs, embed them in word-processing documents, and print them. It's simple. In fact, we'll do one together. Right now I'm writing this text in Microsoft *Word,* but I'm going to leave for a moment to create a graph in *Excel.* Don't go away.

Okay, I'm back. While I was away I typed some data from a 7th-grade class survey of TV viewing into *Excel.* Then I clicked the Chart Wizard button on the toolbar. The Chart Wizard took me step by step through creating a graph, giving me various choices and options. I chose a pie chart with percentages, added a title and some labels, and created a legend. Finally, I selected the graph, copied it, and pasted it right here.

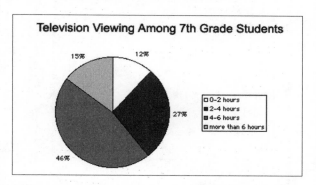

Adult tools such as *Excel* produce business-like graphs and charts, and have many powerful features that can sometimes confuse younger students. If you're looking for a graphing tool for a somewhat younger crowd, try *The Graph Club*, a graphing program by Tom Snyder Productions that's designed specifically for an elementary educational setting.

Graphing Students' Favorite Pets with The Graph Club
With a program like The Graph Club, *you can easily create fun, kid-friendly graphs for your classroom. Turn to page 124 for step-by-step instructions on creating a graph of students' favorite pets with* The Graph Club. *You can download a free demo version of the product from the Tom Snyder Productions Web site.*
www.tomsnyder.com/weaving

Designed for grades K–4, the graphic displays in *The Graph Club* help move students from the concrete environment of manipulatives to the more abstract world of graphs. The difference between what you see in this educational product versus the more business-oriented programs described above can be dramatic. Let's say, for instance, that an elementary class is charting the weather each day at recess time for the month of May.

In the spreadsheet function of *AppleWorks,* which works very much like *Excel,* the raw data and the pictogram might look like this:

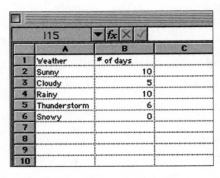 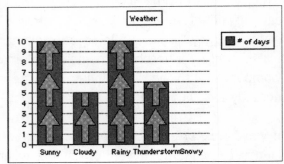

In *The Graph Club,* on the other hand, both the raw data and the picture graph have a more kid-friendly look:

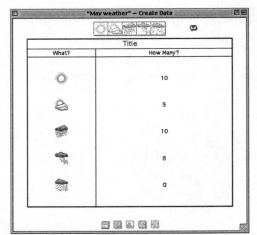 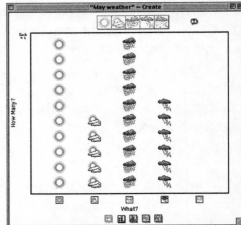

These graphs are cute and friendly, and the interface is simple enough for a young student or a beginning computer-using teacher to use. Plus, *The Graph Club* lets you print graphs poster-size and type notes or stories to print with your graph. Posting these graphs around your room keeps students involved in mathematics and the visual representation of data.

Maps

As a former social studies teacher, I have a special place in my heart for maps. In particular, when I taught ancient history, I loved my set of overlapping map transparencies. The base transparency might have an outline map of Asia Minor. I'd slide an overlapping transparency on top and the civilizations of, say, 400 B.C. appeared. Another layer revealed migrations and battles. The maps were not just helpful, they were essential to help place these civilizations in their geographic contexts. So, I'm a big advocate of having maps on the walls and in kids' hands for studying geography, history, cultures, and anything that has to do with the spread of ideas and technology.

The resources available on CD-ROM and the Internet give you access to maps for just about anything. You can go online and get maps for directions, maps of your community, and even satellite images. One CD-ROM program, *Mapmaker's Toolkit* by Tom Snyder Productions, puts a database of contemporary and historical maps at your fingertips, and then lets you customize them for your own use. You can print your custom maps or create a slide show that illustrates, for example, changing borders or migrations.

Let me offer a couple of quick examples. The contentious election of 2000 between George W. Bush and Al Gore provided educators with a golden opportunity to highlight the U.S. electoral system. With *Mapmaker's Toolkit,* you could create an electoral college map to hand out to students. In class, you could ask students to play the role of campaign strategists. Which states are most important to carry to win the election? Where should the candidates spend the most time? Can the class predict which states will go Democrat and which Republican? Will any go to Ralph Nader? *Mapmaker's Toolkit* lets you easily color code each state: red for Bush, blue for Gore, yellow too close to call. And when the election is over, you can quickly create a map that shows the actual results. Each map can be printed on a single sheet of paper, with or without the legend, or poster size. What a helpful tool to support your efforts.

Try out these other geography and mapping software:

Make-a-Map 3-D
(Sunburst Technology)

My First Amazing World Explorer (DK Interactive Learning)

Neighborhood Map Machine
(Tom Snyder Productions)

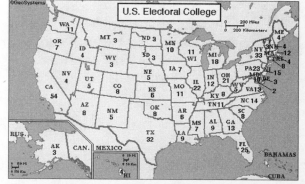

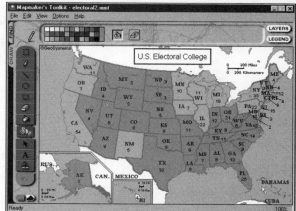

Easily customize current and historical maps with Mapmaker's Toolkit.

Awards

As a high school teacher I didn't reward my students with certificates and stickers. They were too cool for that kind of stuff. My son, on the other hand, cherishes the little awards he brings home from elementary school. Awards are one more example of cool stuff you can make on a computer and use in your classroom.

The educational versions of software packages like *AppleWorks* and Microsoft *Office* typically contain templates of different kinds of certificates that you can modify and print for your students. You can also find specific certificate-, banner-, and even sticker-making programs in various educational software catalogs. Combine these simple programs with some clip art and you can create and decorate certificates for reading a certain number of books, writing a poem, competing in a math contest, participating in geography and spelling bees, and so on. You can make stickers or award cards to distribute to students who turn their work in on time, use a vocabulary word, or who propose a scientific hypothesis to explain some observed behavior.

An award template from AppleWorks

Of course, what students truly value is YOU giving those awards to them. It's the recognition from a caring person that the student respects that children cherish, not the fact that the award came out of the computer. As we look at how the computer can be a powerful tool to support classroom learning, I feel compelled to offer these periodic reminders that you, the teacher, are the most important ingredient to a successful school experience for your students.

I've described just a few of the many ways you can use your computer and printer outside of the classroom to help you teach and motivate your students inside the classroom. Enrolling parental support in your classroom efforts, keeping better tabs on student performance, planning great lessons, and creating cool stuff to hand out and put up on the walls are all wonderful outcomes that technology can support. The computer and Internet offer tools that can help you be better prepared with less effort. It may take some initial extra time to learn the tools, but when you see the benefits, you'll know that the effort was worth it. Even if your classroom computer does nothing more than help you to get ready to teach your students, it will have accomplished a great deal, because that's the relationship that matters.

Using Technology Inside the Classroom

A computerized gradebook is just the tip of the iceberg. There are so many other ways that teachers can use computers, and so much quality educational software out there, whether it's drill and skill, reference, or interactive software. As long as it meets the needs of your students and facilitates learning, it's going to be beneficial. But computers can't do it all. The teacher has to be the facilitator.

Susan Schoessel
Assistant Principal
Terry Elementary School
Little Rock, Arkansas

Using Technology Inside the Classroom

In the 1980s, the early years of the personal computer, computer makers like Atari and Commodore designed their advertisements to strike fear into the hearts of parents who hadn't yet purchased a home computer for their children to use. In one commercial, a computerless boy stood sadly at a train station as a train full of his more computer-savvy peers chugged off to college. The clear message: Without a computer, your child will get left behind.

Today, high-tech skills are in demand in the work force more than ever before. Parents and educators feel an urgent need to expose children to technology so they can later compete in the job market. In some low-income urban and rural communities where home computers still aren't prevalent, schools may provide the only opportunity for children to get their hands on the machines. Quite a few schools have responded by making student computer training an explicit goal. In their already busy schedules, teachers are being asked to allot time and find ways for students to learn and use technology.

While getting students comfortable and familiar with technology is an important goal, I'm not sure that it's the most important use of classroom technology. Computer technology changes constantly. The Timex Sinclair and Radio Shack Model III computers I used in the early 1980s bear little resemblance to the computer that sits on my desk now. A mouse? A desktop? Double-clicking? None of this vocabulary existed when I first encountered the technology. Everything I learned initially about using computers I had to relearn with the next generation of hardware and software, and then relearn again with the subsequent generation. The development of the Internet, voice recognition, artificial intelligence, and small, targeted devices like personal digital assistants (PDAs) and MP3 players will lead to yet more periods of relearning. Exposure to a moment in the computer's evolutionary life seems less valuable for students than learning how to adapt to the inevitable change that technology brings. While getting students comfortable with technology is important, more critical is teaching them the skills for critical thinking, communication, and lifelong learning. These will serve students much better than knowledge about specific technologies as they make their way in a constantly changing world.

So rather than having students use the computer as an end in itself, we need to give another purpose to computer use by students and in classrooms. When I was a teacher, I first considered what I wanted my students to learn before planning a lesson. Then I determined what teaching strategy and tools I could use to

Forget about finding a way to use the computer for a minute. What are your educational goals?

best enable that learning. I never wondered, "Hmmm, what can I do with the chalkboard tomorrow?" Nor was I ever tempted by the electronic wizardry of the overhead projector to find a way to weave a lesson around it. My use of these tools came only after I had identified my educational goals and selected a pedagogical strategy for attacking them. So, that's where I'll begin here. Forget about finding a way to use the computer for a minute. What are your educational goals? What kinds of things do you want happening inside your classroom? What are your goals for student learning?

Most states have curriculum frameworks that describe, to varying degrees of detail, educational goals for each grade level. Most teachers also have goals for their students that go beyond the standards. They want their students to be thoughtful decision makers, responsible group members, and lifelong learners. I'd like to group all these various goals into four general categories of educational objectives and then explore how technology can help you support those objectives. These four categories aren't as specific as, say, Bloom's Taxonomy of Educational Objectives, but they are meaningful and easy to manage.

1) **Content Acquisition.** There is a lot of information we simply want our children to know and remember. Some of that information, like the multiplication table or the alphabet, provides a foundation for further learning. Other types of content knowledge, such as spelling rules, grammar, or order of mathematical operations, are part of knowing the "rules of the game" in language arts and math. Some historical and geographical knowledge might be considered essential for citizens of our country and members of our culture to have.

2) **Skill Mastery.** Students learn skills by repeating them again and again. The more students practice adding, subtracting, dividing, and multiplying, the more adept they become at those skills. My saxophone-playing son practices every night to become adept at moving his fingers over the instrument. With repetition, the skill of making the correct notes come out of the instrument becomes almost automatic. The same holds true for problem solving, reading, and writing.

3) **Concept Understanding.** While content is information that students learn and recall, conceptual understanding allows students to create new information. For example, a person who knows the notes and has the skill to use a saxophone can play music; a person who also understands music theory can apply that understanding to create new music. Understanding math concepts empowers students to solve problems for which they have not learned a specific formula. Understanding science concepts enables students to infer and draw conclusions from new data, and so on.

4) Other Good Stuff. I know that I should have a better name for this category, but it really is a bit of a catch-all. It includes all those wonderful "intangibles" that make someone a valuable member of a team. Teamwork, empathy, sympathy, understanding, citizenship, civility, and the ability to listen and communicate can be grouped into this category. Businesses want the workers they hire to possess these traits along with a good attitude and a willingness and ability to keep learning. Teachers want to help their students develop these characteristics. The items under this heading rarely show up in state curriculum frameworks and can't be measured on standardized tests. However, that doesn't mean they aren't critically important.

When you think about it, the four categories I've described above don't just apply to learning that takes place in school. Anytime you're learning something new, these categories can be applied. For example, as I've watched my son learn to play baseball, I've noticed that there is a lot of content he needed to learn. He needed to learn the rules of the game. What's an out? How do you score a run? When can you steal? He also needed to practice the skills of the sport: hitting, throwing, and catching. He needed to have a conceptual understanding of the game to be able to apply strategy. When is it best to bunt? When runners are on base and the ball is hit to him, where should he throw it? Where should he position himself in the field? He also needed all that other good stuff — listening to the coach, supporting his teammates, and other "intangibles" that make him a good team member.

In the following pages, I'll discuss the role that technology can play to support learning in the context of meeting these four objectives. One at a time, I'll explore which pedagogies best match the objectives of each category, and give examples of relevant software that can help your students acquire content, master skills, understand concepts, and develop the intangibles. You'll discover that the computer can be much more than a back-of-the-room diversion for students. It can be a powerful instructional tool that you can weave into your daily agenda to help you meet your instructional objectives.

My grouping of our collective educational goals draws from my experiences and thinking about learning, but it remains, for me, a work in progress. I fully expect that you'll find lots of exceptions to my rules. Great! Let me know about them. If they provoke thought and lead to deeper understanding, I'll be more than satisfied (and I'll have reason to write another book).

The computer can be a powerful instructional tool that you can weave into your daily agenda to help you meet your instructional objectives.

That "Other Good Stuff"

With all the rich content and important skills we have to cover to meet the requirements of the state standards, we often find ourselves short of time for this other good stuff.

You might have noticed that my scheme for organizing educational goals has three neatly defined categories and one catch-all group. So why am I starting with the catch-all group? Shouldn't I wait until I've covered content acquisition, skill mastery, and concept development before getting to the "other good stuff"? The problem is this: if we save all this other good stuff until the end, we may not get to it. Because it's not in the curriculum or measured on the tests, the intangibles can easily get left behind. With all the rich content and important skills we have to cover to meet the requirements of the state standards, we often find ourselves short of time for this *other* good stuff. Consequently, I want to deal with this category up front. Let's define it and get a good sense of what it involves. Then maybe we can find a way to weave this *other* good stuff into the pursuit of the mandated good stuff. As we consider the other three categories I'll look for ways that you can get a two-for-one deal. Students acquire content *and* develop teamwork at the same time.

Every year the National Association of Colleges and Employers (NACE) surveys employers about the job market, and asks what they are looking for in their employees and new hires. Take a guess what the *Job Outlook 2001* survey revealed as the top-five characteristics employers seek in new hires. Go ahead and guess. It's more fun that way. I can wait.

Okay, here they are: communication skills, honesty/integrity, teamwork skills, interpersonal skills, and motivation/initiative.[27] Now, you might be hard-pressed to find this impressive list of "other good stuff" in your state's curriculum frameworks, and these skills certainly won't be measured by any standardized test. Yet here are these "intangibles" at the top of the list of skills employers want.

In fact, we all want our young people to develop these characteristics. The traits that make someone a valued and valuable employee closely resemble the traits that make someone a cherished family member, a treasured member of the community, and an all-around good person. This other good stuff is the stuff that drove the common school movement shortly after the founding of our nation. Our early leaders wanted and needed a citizenry dedicated to the principles of democracy. Two hundred years ago the educational system in the United States didn't strive to meet the economic needs of businesses; it prepared citizens for the political needs of a fledgling democracy. Those educational goals remain important today. As a teacher I wanted to develop these characteristics in my students, and as a parent I want my child to exhibit these traits.

So, how do we go about teaching them? What classroom practices best support the transmission and acquisition of characteristics like integrity, teamwork, and motivation? Direct instruction, such as a lecture, can help convey the importance of these skills, but that mode of teaching doesn't build these traits. For students to learn teamwork and gain strong interpersonal and communication skills, for them to appreciate the value of honesty and hard work, they have to experience it. So group work, cooperative learning, collaborative projects, and discussions are all important teaching strategies to employ in pursuit of this other good stuff. Using these instructional methods when teaching core content, skills, or concepts can help to reinforce these valued but peripheral objectives.

Great Class Discussions

One of the few subject areas where social skills like citizenship and civility can be addressed directly is in social studies. Tackling, say, a controversial historical or contemporary issue presents students with an opportunity to learn how to assess and respond to conflicting opinions, exercise good listening and communication skills, directly address the roles of citizens and officials in a community, develop critical decision-making skills, and acquire some important content as well.

As I write this, our nation is reeling from the unthinkable terrorist attacks on the World Trade Center towers and the Pentagon. Although the horror of these acts is unmatched in U.S. history, the situation reminds me of my experience teaching high school social studies during the Iranian hostage crisis. The Shah of Iran had been overthrown and American workers were being held hostage in the U.S. embassy in Tehran. People across the nation were riveted to their televisions waiting for the next bit of news. Nightly updates from ABC News continued for so long that the program *Nightline* was born. My students needed a forum to discuss these gripping events, and I seized the opportunity to encourage thoughtful behavior and even infuse some curricular content.

I initiated a class discussion by asking students to role-play a decision maker facing this critical situation. "You're President Jimmy Carter," I began. "The hostages are in Iran. What do you do?" Can you predict the students' immediate response? "Nuke 'em!" I had hoped for something a bit more thoughtful. "I don't think that will get the hostages back safely," I reminded them. With some pushing and pulling, a more informed discussion began to take shape. "I think we should take aggressive action, like Teddy Roosevelt," one student finally offered. "No," another countered, "the country is isolationist, like it was under Wilson." Wow! When a discussion clicks, it really clicks. Students were thinking through the consequences of their suggestions. They were listening to each other. They were even using history to support their ideas. When the bell rang to end the class, the discussion poured into the hallway. Some students continued strands of it in the cafeteria and even at home at the dinner table.

Students were thinking through the consequences of their suggestions. They were listening to each other. They were even using history to support their ideas.

Unfortunately, not all my discussions met with such rich success. Coaxing broad student participation, managing impolite behavior, correcting misinformation, and keeping everyone focused is difficult. When it goes well, though, students can practice interpersonal and communication skills, work together as a team, discuss responsible behavior, learn how to disagree, and become motivated to push their thinking further, all while reinforcing important content. And, believe it or not, the computer can help.

A series of role-playing software packages called *Decisions, Decisions* (Tom Snyder Productions) can help you generate this type of informed discussion and decision making in the classroom. Unlike a lot of educational software, which is designed to be used by students individually, *Decisions, Decisions* is designed to be used by a teacher leading a group discussion. The CD-ROM titles in the series deal with topics ranging from colonization to immigration to ancient empires. In addition, an Internet version of the program (called *Decisions, Decisions Online*) focuses specifically on current events and issues, including gun control, cloning, and juvenile crime. I'll focus this example on the *Decisions, Decisions: The Environment* CD-ROM.

The *Decisions, Decisions* software can be used in a variety of ways. Four students can gather around a computer in the back of a classroom or in a lab. Teams of students can rotate turns at a single computer in the classroom. Or you can mix small-group and large-group discussions. That's my favorite method and the one I'm going to describe. The physical setup is simple. I usually employ a single computer sitting on my desk or on a cart in the front of the room. You don't need a display system, although it's fine to use one. During the discussion, I act as the interface between the class and the computer. That position makes it easier for me to orchestrate large-group discussions. The computer is there primarily to push the discussion along and help me manage the activity.

· · · · · · · · · ·

Creating Cooperative Groups

Sorting a classroomful of students with diverse backgrounds, reading levels, and personalities into cooperative groups that will work well together is something of an art form. Turn to page 127 for some tips on creating effective cooperative groups.

I begin by dividing the class into teams of four students, taking care to create teams that are a balanced mix of genders, ethnicities, personalities, and abilities. *Decisions, Decisions* comes with seven copies each of four different information booklets, known as advisor briefing books. While students all assume the same role (in the case of *The Environment* title, the mayor of a small town), each member of a team gets a different book filled with advice from one of the four advisors: a campaign manager, an environmentalist, a scientist, and an economist. Students will share and debate the conflicting advice in the books as they work their way through an environmental crisis. That crisis is introduced to the class through an engaging slide show that plays from the software.

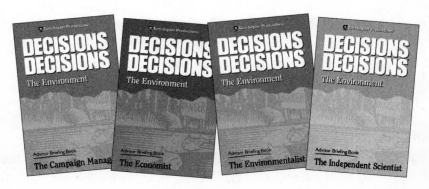

"Dead fish!" The headline glares at you from your desk. The danger forced you, the mayor of Alpine, to close Snyder Pond. Could the nearby dump be polluting the pond and killing the fish? Or is it some other cause, like acid rain? Many people suspect the town dump. Who knows what Malaco, the mining company, is dumping there? Are Malaco and its jobs really good for Alpine? What if the company seeks to mine beautiful Gab's Gully? You're the mayor, and it's an election year. What should you do?

Decisions, Decisions begins with an engaging slide show.

After viewing the setup of the story on the CD-ROM students' first task before making any decisions is to rank the "mayor's" four goals: win reelection, protect the environment, hold down costs, and preserve Alpine's economy. Students turn to their briefing books to hear from their advisors. Each advisor summarizes the dilemma from his or her unique perspective. Taking into account these conflicting viewpoints, the group must turn the four goals into a set of priorities, from most important to least important. I usually require students to complete this ranking exercise independently before initiating any group discussions. That way they get invested in a point of view, so that when they do start talking, they have a lot more to say. Most students are quickly off and running, and I'm free to move among the groups that were slow to get started. After a few prompts, they too are on their way. The discussions are great.

"We've got to make the environment our number-one priority!"

"But the economist says that Malaco provides most of the jobs in the town, and the economy isn't doing well."

"Hey, according to the campaign manager, if we don't get reelected we can't do anything."

Gradually, the teams reach some sort of agreement on the mayor's priorities. I then turn the class's attention back to the computer. In this mode of play, the software asks for one set of priorities, so we now have to reach a class consensus. I ask for one team's priority rankings, and then hands start shooting up around the room. A whole-class discussion is under way. Teams typically start out with simple negotiation. "We'll agree to make protecting the environment the number-one priority if the economy is number two." "No way. Getting reelected is the most important." Students soon realize that they need to be more persuasive. They begin building arguments, supported by evidence from the advisor briefings and elsewhere, to convince one another to adopt a particular point of view. After a great amount of wrangling and some close votes, you will eventually end up with a set of class priorities.

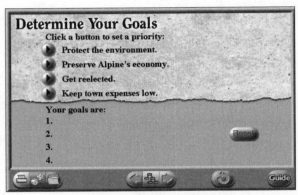

The first step is to determine your goals.

Teacher Tip

Our 7th-grade classes used *Decisions, Decisions: Colonization* as an introductory activity to a small-group project that we found on the Internet. "Create-a-Colony" enabled the students to create either a colony from the past (Colonial America, which is part of our 7th-grade social studies curriculum) or the future (on another planet or under the sea). We used *Decisions, Decisions: Colonization* as a whole-class activity to introduce and reinforce necessary concepts: what is a colony, a constitution, a democracy, teamwork, and cooperation.

Each group of students had to develop a name for its colony, a flag, national anthem, constitution, and journal entry for a typical colonist. The student groups did all of their work during class time in social studies and in the computer lab. They shared their presentations with their classmates and helped to develop a grading rubric.

This project allowed students to experience some of the challenges and frustrations faced by the original colonists. It exceeded our expectations. Each and every student participated and came away from the project with a better understanding of the concepts of colonization, government, laws, and cooperative effort as well as a sense of pride and accomplishment.

Cathy Fitzgerald & Rickey Moroney
St. Agnes Cathedral School
Rockville Center, New York

Setting priorities is just the first step of the program. As the class moves into the main decision-making phase, I continue to use this same organizational style. The program offers students three options for what action they'll take as mayor. Once again, the advisors reappear to point students back to their briefing books for conflicting bits of

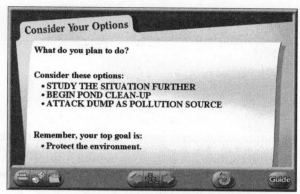

Students choose one of the three options.

advice and relevant information. In their small groups, students read the advice, share the information with their teammates, and then debate which action to take. I then select a team to summarize its decision. Another class discussion follows. On it goes for five decisions. It's a fantastic exchange, full of the content you're covering in your curriculum, along with a terrific level of enthusiasm from students. Karen Hague, a teacher at Lancaster High School in California, says the issues raised in *Decisions, Decisions: The Environment* resonated with her students, and that led to great discussions. She says, "The environment is very important to kids. They see that this is their future at stake, and they want to make sure they have one! So they took these decisions seriously and were passionate about this activity."

Decisions, Decisions Online, which is available both on the Internet and on CD-ROM, follows a similar structure for engaging students in thoughtful discussions. In addition to debating the issues with their class, students can also see how their counterparts across the country voted on the issue, even breaking the results down by region. (Shown are voting results from *Decisions, Decisions Online: Gun Control.*) Using the online bulletin board, students can also carry on their conversations with other students from around the world.

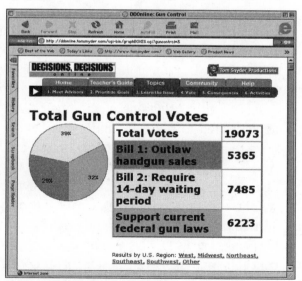

With Decisions, Decisions Online, *your class can vote on key issues.*

Teacher Tip

I use *Decisions, Decisions Online* to give students practice finding the main idea in reading, and retelling it orally. First, we watch the introductory video as a class. Then students take their advisor briefings home to read. At home, they share the main idea of their briefing with their parents. I think this is an important connection because it gives parents and children a chance to connect and express their feelings about important issues. When students come back the next day, they discuss the issue in groups. I'm always impressed at how passionately students argue their advisors' points of view, even if it is one the student doesn't share. Each student knows that it's his or her job to convey their advisor's point of view to everybody else so that the group can make a decision. They love playing the part and they take it seriously.

Brenda Lium
6th-grade teacher
Agassiz Middle School
Fargo, North Dakota

I love the *Decisions, Decisions* approach. It begins with students working alone, ensuring individual accountability; then it requires students to work in small groups where everyone has to contribute. Finally, the teacher gets to pull all the pieces together in a large-group discussion. It's fun and tremendously educational for students, plus it creates a very rewarding classroom experience for teachers.

Decisions, Decisions is a great tool for sparking student-to-student interaction and building teamwork, interpersonal, and communication skills. The computer drives the discussion and helps you manage the activity, but it is not the center of attention; the kids and their ideas are. Here's what one teacher wrote to the designers after using one of the titles: "As I turned the computer on, my students waited to see color and magic light up the screen. How delighted they were to find that all the color and magic came from them and their ideas!"

One challenge I mentioned earlier is how to give these *other* skills significant weight and time with all the pressure of covering what's articulated in the curriculum and assessed on the tests. How can you justify taking time from the high-stakes goals for these *other* ones? Maybe you don't have to. Core content, concepts, and skills can be taught in conjunction with this other good stuff, and software like *Decisions, Decisions* can help.

Content Acquisition

A number of years ago, I attended a workshop on cooperative learning at an Association of Supervision and Curriculum Development conference. The presenters lectured for close to an hour, and offered reams of data confirming that people learn better when they learn cooperatively. After the session I approached the presenters and asked, "If cooperative learning is so powerful, why didn't you use it in this workshop?" Their response: "We had a lot to cover in a short amount of time."

Sometimes efficiency matters. When you have a lot of information to convey in a limited period of time, direct instruction looks like a pretty good instructional vehicle. "Here are the facts that you need to know class, and yes, they will be on the test. Learn them." You can't get much more direct and efficient than that. And, in fact, large chunks of the curriculum are made up of the kind of content that could be taught in this manner. This is the type of content — information that students just plain need to remember — that is frequently found on state tests. Here are a couple of examples from the Massachusetts 5th-grade history and social science test from 2001:

Mesopotamia, in the Greek language, means "the land between two rivers." Between which two rivers was Mesopotamia located?

A. Nile and Ganges
B. Tigris and Euphrates
C. Nile and Euphrates
D. Ganges and Huang He (Yellow)

The American colonists who supported King George III during the Revolution were called:

A. Minutemen
B. Federalists
C. Patriots
D. Loyalists

Not surprisingly, social studies, with its combination of historical facts, geographic data, and cultural information demands a great deal of content learning. The vocabulary- and terminology-laden discipline of science also relies heavily on information recall, as these questions from a 2001 Texas biology exam demonstrate:

The human body uses carbohydrates as a –

A. source of energy
B. material for muscle production
C. carrier of oxygen
D. coenzyme of metabolism

Which of these researchers would be most interested in maintaining a healthy deciduous forest?

A. Biochemist
B. Sonographer
C. Toxicologist
D. Ecologist

Even the rich skill domain of math requires some content acquisition. Students, for instance, need to know the multiplication table in order to perform any multiplication task. And they need to be able to recall the meanings of key terms as this sample task from the 2001 8th-grade Florida math test illustrates:

The table below lists seven heavy metals and their atomic weights.

Metal	Atomic Weight
Curium	247
Berkelium	247
Californium	251
Einsteinium	252
Fermium	257
Mendelevium	258
Nobelium	259

What is the difference between the **median** atomic weight and the **mode** atomic weight for these seven metals?

If you can't recall what "median" and "mode" mean, you're going to have a tough time responding to this question.

We can all recall fundamental content we learned in school, and we can also probably recall some of the more interesting devices that helped us remember it. I taught my son the ABC song to help him remember the alphabet. That same song helped me memorize my ABCs. The songs of *Schoolhouse Rock* helped me and some of my students remember bits of content in math, grammar, and American history. I think I can still sing a good part of "Conjunction Junction." Flashcards helped me learn the multiplication table, and years later they helped my son. Spelling bees helped motivate me to learn spelling rules and memorize the odd spellings of many words.

Another strong memory-enhancing mechanism is drama. Children, and adults for that matter, will remember even the minutest details from a compelling story, whether the content is historical, mathematical, or scientific. Students can see the names Paul Revere and Sam Adams in a textbook or on a time line in the classroom, but when they read *Johnny Tremain,* these characters and their roles in history become unforgettable.

Technology can help you support content acquisition in powerful ways. Multimedia authoring tools can make direct presentation of content visually compelling and more memorable for students. Well-designed computer games can make the repetition of content fun. And interactive software can engage students in content-rich narrative situations that give dramatic context and meaning to the information they're acquiring.

Technology can help you support content acquisition in powerful ways.

Compelling Presentations

Leaf through the pages of an airline magazine or another journal directed toward businesspeople and you will likely find numerous ads for large-scale display devices for computers. Printing your graphs, time lines, and other creations on paper is just one way of sharing your ideas with an audience. A second method of sharing involves going straight from the computer to the big screen. As the business world has discovered, one advantage of bypassing the printer is that you can edit your work at any time without having to reprint your presentation on paper or transparencies. A second advantage is that you can display colors beautifully and with ease. Color printers may be inexpensive, but color copiers aren't. Most schools don't have the resources for teachers to make color handouts for each student. In the long run, a projection system could be more affordable than color reproductions.

••••••••••
***Large-Scale
Display Systems***
*The market for presentation
devices is large and continues to
evolve rapidly, making newer,
better, and cheaper options
available to you. Turn to page
129 for some tips on choosing
and using display devices in
your classroom.*

Another advantage of computer-aided presentations in the classroom is that they can be dynamic — you can change the information you're displaying during your presentation. The graphs you display from the computer, for example, don't have to be static images. You can actually use a graphing program during your presentation and change the information as you talk. This enables you to explain not just the end results but how you got them as well. With the right kind of software, you could even add a few fancy transitions and effects to your computer presentation. A little color and dazzle can go a long way in holding your audience's attention. The power is in your hands…assuming you have the right equipment. Whether you connect your computer to a television monitor with an inexpensive scan-converter device, or go all out for an LCD palette, a dynamic computer-aided presentation can go a long way in helping your students understand and remember the content you're presenting.

Once you've got your presentation hardware arranged, you can begin to think about what kinds of presentations you want to give. For convenience, I'd like to divide presentations into two categories: linear and nonlinear presentations. Whether it's a movie, a slide show, or a lecture, a linear presentation always follows the same path. A nonlinear presentation doesn't have to follow the same path. In a nonlinear presentation you can change your mind mid-sentence and pursue a different line of thinking. Many of my presentations as a teacher were nonlinear, but not because I planned them that way! On the contrary, I often planned what I expected to be an incredibly clarifying explanation only to look out at a sea of blank faces. Quickly I'd shift gears and try a new explanation, always looking for the words and examples that would connect with my students. In fact, the best lectures, whether linear or nonlinear, are interactive. You ask questions of your students to make sure of their understanding; they ask clarifying questions of you. Those student-teacher interactions can be the richest and most valuable parts of any presentation. In the last couple of years I've found the phrase "interactive lecture" sprinkled liberally through the literature on current classroom practice. Frontal teaching doesn't have to be a one-way conversation.

Linear Presentations: Multimedia Slide Shows

The slide show is a classic method of linear presentation, but the computer has given it a new twist. Programs like Microsoft *PowerPoint* and *AppleWorks* make it easy to construct slide shows. I've used both programs to create presentations for speeches and for classes I teach.

With *AppleWorks* I construct my presentation through a word processor. Each page of the document becomes a "slide" in the slide show. I format the text and cut and paste graphics to make each page clear, concise, and attractive. I can even attach *QuickTime* movies or audio clips to a page. When I have completed the pages, I switch to the program's slide-show mode. In this mode I can pick a border, adjust the background color, reorganize the order of the pages, and determine how the slide show should advance.

You can create slide shows with AppleWorks.

• • • • • • • • • •

Creating a Classroom Rules Slide Show with PowerPoint

A multimedia slide show is a fun way to capture students' attention and emphasize important points. Turn to page 131 for step-by-step instructions on creating a basic PowerPoint slide show, reprinted from the book PowerPoint Workshop for Teachers by Janet Caughlin.

Sally Donahue, who teaches high school social studies in Burlington, Kansas, uses Microsoft *PowerPoint* to create slide shows for her class. Since kids watch a lot of TV, she says, they are naturally drawn to a visual medium and they pay attention. Sally adds graphics, sounds, and animations to keep students focused on her presentations and to accommodate the learning styles of students who are visual and auditory learners. *PowerPoint* has all the features of *AppleWorks* and more, including page layout templates for different kinds of slides. You can add fun transitions from slide to slide, and it's especially easy to add multimedia elements. You can also attach elements from other programs, for example a *KidPix* drawing or an *Excel* graph. Change the data in your *Excel* file and the updated graph will automatically appear in your *PowerPoint* presentation. Another nice feature is the Slide Sorter View. This thumbnail-size overview of your slides makes it easy to reorder and edit a presentation.

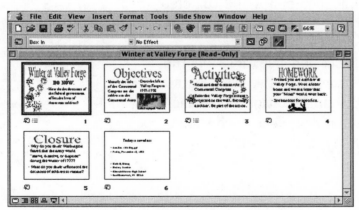

PowerPoint's *slide sorter view makes it easy to organize slides.*

Teacher Tip

Every day I create a *PowerPoint* slide show because it helps the visual learner. When they enter the classroom, kids automatically look at the TV screen to see the daily *PowerPoint* presentation. The first slide is a Do Now activity. Students sit down, open their notebooks, and complete the activity *now*. For example, in the Winter at Valley Forge presentation, students answer the question, "How do the decisions of the federal government affect the lives of American soldiers?"

Next, I show what the students will learn that day (objectives).

The third slide shows the activities of the day. This slide is left up until the activities have been completed. There are two activities in the Winter at Valley Forge lesson. First students read about and discuss the role of the Continental Congress. At the end of the discussion, I project pictures of Valley Forge on the wall using transparencies and an overhead projector. Students use the knowledge gained during the discussion to role-play various characters in scenes at Valley Forge. This makes history come alive for them.

Next, I show the Homework slide. Students are required to write the homework assignment in their agenda books and complete it by the next class period.

As a closure activity, I project discussion questions on the TV screen. These discussion questions center on the day's learnings. The final slide is a reminder of the presentation file name and date it was used, so I can use it again next year. Each slide show is printed and turned in as part of my lesson plans.

Ruth Chang
8th-grade history teacher
Churchill Junior High School/Smith Annex
East Brunswick, New Jersey

Winter at Valley Forge
DO NOW:
· How do the decisions of the federal government affect the lives of American soldiers?

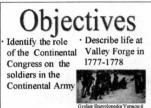

Objectives
· Identify the role of the Continental Congress on the soldiers in the Continental Army
· Describe life at Valley Forge in 1777-1778

Grolier Encyclopedia Version 6

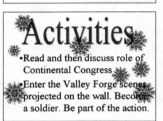

Activities
•Read and then discuss role of Continental Congress
•Enter the Valley Forge scenes projected on the wall. Become a soldier. Be part of the action.

HOMEWORK
· Pretend you are a soldier at Valley Forge. Write a letter home and write a letter that your "Mom" would write back.
· See handout for specifics.

Closure
· Why do you think Washington feared that the army would "starve, dissolve, or disperse" during the winter of 1777?
· What do you think influenced the decisions of soldiers to remain?

Today is saved as:
· Am Rev 15th Day.ppt
· Friday, November 18, 1998

· Ruth D. Chang
· History Teacher
· Churchill Junior High School
· East Brunswick, NJ 08816

Linear Presentations: *TimeLiner*

In addition to slide shows, you can build presentations with content-specific software. Earlier, I discussed how you can use the program *TimeLiner* to create time lines to print out and post around your classroom. You can also use *TimeLiner* to create dynamic presentations. For example, let's say you're teaching U.S. History and your class has been studying World War II. You've got a nifty research project lined up that will engage your students in investigating the U.S.'s decision to drop the atomic bomb on Japan, but first you want to give students a general overview of the events that led up to this decision. This content — the events of the war — could efficiently be delivered through direct instruction, such as a lecture. However, you'd like things to be a bit livelier, and more memorable, than your voice alone can convey.

You open *TimeLiner* and begin typing in important events: the bombing of Pearl Harbor, the battle of Iwo Jima, D-Day, Germany's surrender, and the dropping of the bomb. The order in which you enter the events doesn't matter; *TimeLiner* puts them in chronological order and proportionally spaces them. Now, you can easily attach some multimedia to those events. President Roosevelt's stirring speech after the attack on Pearl Harbor galvanized the country. That would be good to include. So would some images of the devastation of the bombing. You continue to add media and Internet links to enliven your presentation and emphasize the points you wish to make.

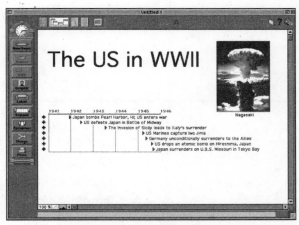

TimeLiner *makes it easy to organize events.*

With the click of a button, you can present your time line in slide-show format. Each event on your time line becomes a slide, projecting text, images, and including multimedia and Web links. On the slide shown here, the Web Link button links to a site with dramatic pictures of the attack. With the audio controller you can play a portion of Roosevelt's speech. You now have both a printable time line, and a dynamic audiovisual presentation to reinforce the content you're trying to convey to your students.

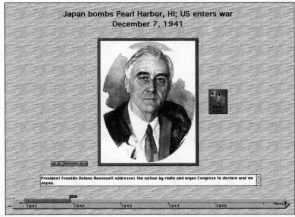

With TimeLiner 5.0, *you can create a multimedia slide show.*

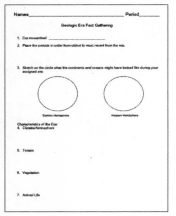

I find *TimeLiner* very helpful in teaching my students about Earth's history and helping them recognize that change occurs constantly and slowly over time. First, I assign pairs of students to gather data and research particular geologic eras. I distribute a Geologic Era Fact-Gathering Worksheet for students to record data for their time line. During their research students record a few pages that have pictures they would like to scan and include in their time line. I also feel it is important for students to draw or sketch an original piece of artwork for the time line. Each pair of students presents its time line in Slide Show mode, while the other students take notes. Finally, students merge their time lines of individual eras to make a complete geologic time line.

Wende Schweizer
Middle-grade science teacher
Educational Technology Center
Kennesaw State University
Kennesaw, Georgia

This kind of linear presentation can be at your fingertips as the power of the technology becomes increasingly familiar and comfortable. Before you take the leap of bringing dynamic software tools into the classroom, however, let me offer a word of advice: Make sure you know the software well. Teaching with a tool is like singing while playing a musical instrument. If you have to stop one while doing the other, the power of the performance is severely diminished. Not only that, your relationship with your audience is compromised. I've seen this happen in classrooms even with a tool as mundane as the chalkboard. In fact, many teachers prefer an overhead projector to the chalkboard for the very reason that they can write without turning their backs on their students. This was one of the key features touted by the innovators who introduced the overhead projector to schools in the 1960s. As a new teacher, I felt angry and disappointed that classroom management was such a concern for many teachers. If teachers couldn't turn their backs on their students, I concluded they must be bad teachers. A good teacher, I assumed, would have gotten his or her students so excited about learning that discipline wouldn't be an issue. Of course, it didn't take me long to realize how difficult teaching can be. I grew to appreciate the value of eye contact and personal presence. Any educational technology you use should enhance, rather than hinder, the relationships you are trying to create in your classroom.

Nonlinear Presentations: *HyperStudio*

Once you're comfortable with a given software program, you might consider using it in a less structured and predictable manner. Instead of determining a step-by-step path you'll follow in a presentation, you can allow your students' questions to govern the path of the presentation. As I mentioned earlier, I often found myself shifting strategies midstream as input from students gave me a clearer idea of what they did and did not understand. With a slide show, options for changing your mind are limited once you begin the presentation. Other software, however, can give you the flexibility to deviate from your predetermined linear path.

One very popular, general nonlinear presentation tool is *HyperStudio,* published by Knowledge Adventure. Like *PowerPoint* and the slide-show mode in *AppleWorks,* this tool allows you to piece together text, images, movies, and sounds representing any content you like. Instead of pages or slides, *HyperStudio* stores content on "cards." Each card can have buttons connecting it to other cards. In a linear presentation, each card would connect only to the cards that preceded and followed it (like a slide show). In a nonlinear presentation a card might have several connections — called "links" — representing the different paths you might choose to follow. If you can anticipate where students might have trouble, you can use these links to build in optional explanations and alternative anecdotes just in case you need them.

That knowledge of alternatives and anticipation of trouble grows with experience. I know, for example, that some students (and many adults) have a tough time comprehending the concept of gravity. After all, the presence of an invisible force so weak that it is barely perceptible, and yet so strong that it holds our solar system together and our bodies to the planet, can be confusing. To explain gravity, a main presentation path might contain images of rockets, falling objects, and graphs of weight variations from planet to planet. Since we see the effects of gravity mainly on a planetary level, describing it from a planetary point of view makes sense. But planets are awfully big. Such an explanation could leave students with the misconception that only planets have gravity. In fact, all objects with

Creating a Rain Forest Presentation with HyperStudio
If you have HyperStudio you can quickly get started creating your own nonlinear presentations. Turn to page 142 for a tutorial on creating a rainforest presentation with HyperStudio.

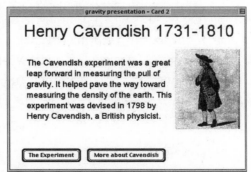

HyperStudio cards have buttons that can link to different places.

mass have gravity. You just need a whole lot of mass to see gravity's effects. So, anticipating possible confusion, you might attach a button to each card in your main *HyperStudio* presentation that allows you to pursue an alternative approach. For example, Henry Cavendish's 1798 experiment showed that a heavy metal ball exerted a small gravitational effect on a smaller object dangling near it from a string. It's a great historical anecdote that can be told with drama and tension.

Toss in some images of the experiment and a picture of Cavendish himself, and you have a nice alternative path. Over time, as you learn more about how your students come to understanding and as you learn more about the subject area, you can attach additional anecdotes to your presentation. Logging the content into this nonlinear authoring tool helps capture accumulated wisdom.

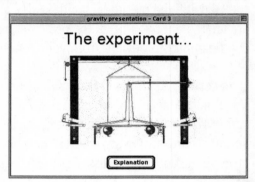

Nonlinear Presentations: *Inspiration*

Alternatively, rather than trying to anticipate confusion and building multiple paths into a presentation, you might consider following a more Socratic method. Instead of a presentation that tells to students, you could create a presentation that elicits from them. Who can tell me one reason why the Civil War began? How many of you think this bar graph shows that a greater number of people believe in aliens than this circle graph does? Do you think that the Tuck family in *Tuck Everlasting* would be happy living forever? We are constantly questioning students, pushing their thinking further and leading them to make connections. Although we're trying to guide students to a certain idea, we want them to be the ones carrying us along. Sometimes a direct, factual question can get the ball rolling; sometimes a more open-ended question is needed. In any case, some computer tools can help you record and illuminate these student-fed discussions as they happen.

As I described earlier, *Inspiration* is a tool that you can use to organize your own thinking process when planning lessons. Many teachers also use it as a dynamic classroom tool to help map students' ideas. Unlike a chalkboard or traditional paper graphic organizers, *Inspiration* allows you to throw ideas up on the screen and then arrange and rearrange them later. Shelley Chabak, a language arts teacher in Decatur, Illinois, says she likes giving her students a chance to figure out how ideas should connect. She says, "When I give my students a reproduced copy of a paper organizer, they're forced to fit things into the structure that I

Creating a K-W-L Web with Inspiration

Inspiration *can be a wonderful tool to track students' growing knowledge throughout a unit. Turn to page 149 for step-by-step instructions on creating a basic What We Know, What We Want to Know, What We've Learned (K-W-L) chart with* Inspiration.

drew beforehand. With *Inspiration,* we can build the graphic organizer together as we put the text in. It helps them focus on how the ideas are connected." As you build an organizer with *Inspiration,* you can solicit from students, prod them to supply facts and opinions, without worrying if the order is perfect. The chalkboard is a marvelous tool for capturing thoughts, but it's tough to erase and rewrite to get the proper organization. A quick look at a literature example will highlight the power of this program.

Suppose your class has just read *Fantastic Mr. Fox* by Roald Dahl. With your computer connected to a television monitor, you launch *Inspiration* and begin a class discussion of the story elements. As students volunteer their ideas you collect their thoughts in the program simply by typing words and phrases. You question, prompt, and reward. Soon, idea bubbles are scattered all over the screen. Then, with the students' help, you begin to connect them. A quick flip to outline mode gives you the chance to see your graphic organizer in traditional outline form. (Try switching back and forth between a graphical and an outline view on your chalkboard!) By the end of the lesson, you have a custom-made graphic organizer that you can print out and copy for students to use when they write summaries of the book.

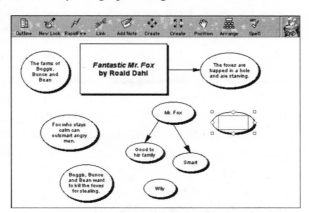

You can place ideas on the screen in any order.

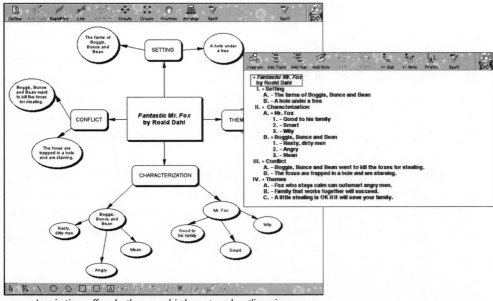

Inspiration *offers both a graphic layout and outline view.*

Inspiration is one of those programs that doesn't just sit in one curriculum area. Although it's a great prewriting tool to help kids get organized, it's not just for English. It can also cross over to social studies, science, and math. In our school, some of the science teachers use it to make flow charts for lab experiments. For each stage of the experiment, they can map out what gets done first, what gets done next, and how the path of the experiment might change based on the results of each step. We also have a math teacher in our building who likes to use *Inspiration* to help students break down word problems. What information do they need to solve the problem? What are the extraneous parts that they don't need? In what order should they do the problem? In all subject areas, *Inspiration* helps teachers and students organize information quickly and easily in a visual way.

Sharon Jackson
Technology integration specialist
Horace Mann Middle School
Franklin, Massachusetts

Initially, a program like *Inspiration* can appear intimidating. It might be…at first. But so were word processors, and now most of us can't imagine writing without one. Take your time. Don't expect to be able to learn the technology unless you have access to it. And once you have access, be patient and have a purpose. To minimize the risk, try *Inspiration* with a lesson about which you already feel very confident. If things don't go well, you can likely still pull it off. Remember, too, that the technology is supposed to help you, and it will.

Nonlinear Presentations: *The Graph Club*

Let me offer one more quick example of a dynamic presentation. Math is a highly visual discipline and one in which the chalkboard can be limiting. Just drawing round circles and straight lines can be a struggle for those of us less adept with chalk. The computer, though, can draw exactly what we want each and every time. And it can dynamically change those drawings based on what we tell it to do.

I've already talked about how easy it is to produce graphs with programs like Microsoft *Excel* and *The Graph Club* that you can distribute to students or post on the wall. You can also use these programs during class to dynamically create graphs with your students' input. One of the many nice features in *The Graph*

Club is the ability to make changes in one graph format and simultaneously see the results in other formats. For example, let's say your first-grade class is planning an end-of-the-year party. Asking for suggestions yields four reasonable choices: a pizza party, a hamburger party, a bring-your-own-treats party, or a trip to the circus. You take a vote, and as you add the raw numbers to one graph, the data can be displayed in up to four other formats simultaneously.

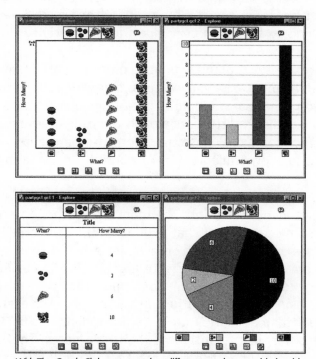

With The Graph Club, *you can view different graph types side by side.*

Based on the bar and pie graphs, the circus looks like an overwhelming favorite, yet the difference between the circus and the pizza party is only four votes. What happens if we throw out burgers and treats and let those six students vote for the remaining two choices? It's easy to find out. Just click the top of the hamburger and treats bars and drag them down to zero. The other three graphs will change accordingly. Now add the results of the new vote by clicking and dragging the bars in the bar graph or the wedges in the circle graph. You could also type the numbers into the table. No matter how you make the changes, the results will be displayed in all the graphs.

With the help of the computer, your students can witness dynamic change in context. They can decide how to celebrate the end of the year while getting a lesson on graphic representation of numbers. It seems very simple, but try doing it on a traditional chalkboard. That's a lot of erasing and redrawing.

Teacher Tip

On the very first day of school my third-grade students are introduced to the pictograph. We graph their birthdays using cutout cakes, and discuss how graphing can help us organize and interpret information more clearly. We start out using only a pictograph, and after several examples the students have the opportunity to create one on their own using specific information.

Once the students have shown mastery on the pictograph, we move on to the bar graph. The students learn the parts of a graph: title, horizontal axis, vertical axis, titles for each axis, and how to number the graph. They learn how to gather data, record it on a tally sheet, and transfer the information to a bar graph. At this time, I gather the students around the computer and give them an introductory lesson with *The Graph Club* program. We use the information presented in class to create a bar graph with the software. I also show students how to translate the data into the different types of graphs.

From this point on, every day when the students come into the room they respond to a question such as "What is your favorite fruit?" on a piece of paper that is dropped into a bucket. Later that day, during our math class, we do a classroom tally sheet on a bulletin board that is set aside specifically for graphing. Four students are then chosen to create a graph on the computer using *The Graph Club* software, while the other students do the same on paper. They must also create a five-question quiz, with an answer key, using the information on the graph. (For example: How many more people were born in December than January?) Not only do students become expert at creating and interpreting graphs, but also they learn a lot about their classmates! This is done on a regular basis until all students have several opportunities to use *The Graph Club*. All of the computer-generated graphs are compiled in a notebook entitled "Everything You Ever Wanted To Know About Our Class."

Colleen R. Moritz
3ʳᵈ-grade teacher
Springfield Elementary School
New Middletown, Ohio

Whether your method is direct instruction or engaging students in a dynamic exchange, there are many ways that your classroom computer can help you with your presentations. Software tools can help you display information in colorful and lively formats for both linear and nonlinear presentations, display and change content dynamically, and can help you lead rich, interactive discussions about any subject with your students. With practice, these powerful tools can provide marvelous accompaniment to your performances. And you can even get the audience to sing along with you.

Memorizing for Fun

When I was teaching I used a game based on the TV show *Jeopardy* to encourage students to remember historical names and dates. I know a number of teachers who employ different kinds of classroom trivia games to entice students to remember content. It usually doesn't take much competition to get students excited. Even the most mundane tasks, like reciting the multiplication table or recalling the events of the American Revolution, take on new urgency among students when points are involved.

Software combines fun gaming with content acquisition quite frequently. The geography software I described in the introduction to this book is a prime example. It rewarded students for correctly matching states and capitals by blowing up New Jersey. Oh, wait a minute — New Jersey only blew up if the students got an answer wrong. As you review this type of software, make sure that it's designed so that the incentives are better for correct answers than for incorrect ones.

You'll find plenty of software to review in this category. Among the initial promises of the educational computer revolution were individualized instruction and fun learning. Mix the fun of video games with curricular content and skills and (the advertisers promised) students would be lining up at the computer to learn. (See the Skill Mastery section on page 78 for more on skill-and-drill software.) The lining up at the computer for this kind of software is particularly true in schools, where the alternative might be a lecture or a book to read. At home, however, where television and real video games vie for children's attention, educational software looks somewhat less attractive to kids. Nonetheless, offering students time to repeatedly "play" with the content you're trying to teach can support this part of your content acquisition agenda.

Offering students time to repeatedly "play" with the content you're trying to teach can support this part of your content acquisition agenda.

For many teachers, game-oriented software can present some logistical challenges for regular classroom use. Most software in this genre is designed for a one-on-one experience. Even when students are assigned to work in pairs or small groups, those who aren't sitting in front of the keyboard and holding the mouse may not have a clear role in the activity. Setting up a schedule for student computer use and clearly defining roles for those not at the controls will help greatly.

It's also important to have some mechanism in place to hold students accountable for their time at the computer. Asking students to complete paper-and-pencil worksheets may not be particularly exciting, but the worksheets at least provide a written record of what students did. You can review the completed work, even at a cursory level. How many assignments have you simply marked with a checkmark

While working on the computer might be more fun for students, make sure you know what they're really accomplishing.

or large 'C'? While working on the computer might be more fun for students, make sure you know what they're really accomplishing. What specific content are students acquiring and reinforcing? Which content is well-embedded in memory and which remains elusive? Can you see what students are doing or at least review a record of their actions? Many educational software titles in this genre store student records, and some allow you to designate specific content or skills to be addressed. At the very least, you should look for software that gives you the equivalent of a checkmark on a worksheet. You want to know what the students reviewed and that they actually did something with it. Without this kind of information, you can't really weave the effort into your curricular agenda.

I promised to try to incorporate examples of activities that not only bolster students' acquisition of core content and skills, but also reinforce intangibles like teamwork and interpersonal communication. *International Inspirer* by Tom Snyder Productions is one example of fun, content-building software that incorporates a cooperative learning technique, sometimes called "mixed-expert grouping." This computer game is designed to be used with your whole class at once, so you don't have to worry about the logistics of who's using the computer when.

With *International Inspirer,* students work in groups of four. Each student on a team receives a unique and essential set of materials. He or she becomes an expert, complementary to the other experts in the group. When the game begins, each member in a team of four receives a different map reference booklet. Thus, on any given team, one player has a map booklet highlighting cultural traits such as religion, education, and household size, while a second manages a set of maps displaying deforestation rates, mammal diversity, and health-related information. A third student has political and economic maps, and a fourth has general data (displayed in graphs) on all the nations. So every member of a team is responsible for different, but essential, data. Only together do the students have all the information they need to succeed.

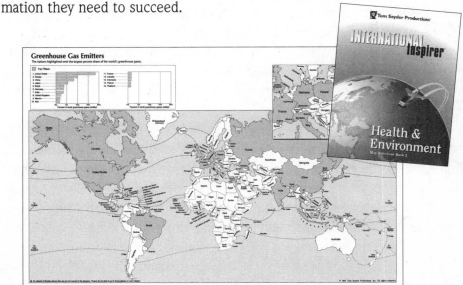

Once you've entered the number of teams into the program, *International Inspirer* displays starting information for you to read to each group. For instance, it might say that Team 1 is starting in Azerbaijan and looking for countries with high precipitation and a high number of immigrants, gaining special bonus points for ending their round in a country with a large land area. Team 2 could be placed in Canada, looking for leading car producers, and nations with high cigarette consumption, with a special bonus awarded for ending up in a densely populated country.

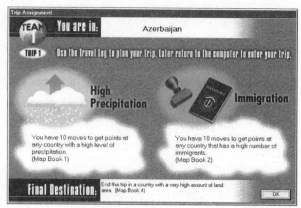

Each team receives an assignment.

With these goals in mind, teams begin planning routes around the world, winning points as they stop in countries that fulfill their assignments. All this planning takes place on paper as students work at their seats, sharing the information from their maps. Everyone on a team has information that can help maximize points.

When they're ready, team members type their moves into the computer, await the results, and then receive their next assignment. When they return to their seats, another team takes its turn at the computer. I've managed 35 students in this lively interactive group experience with a single computer.

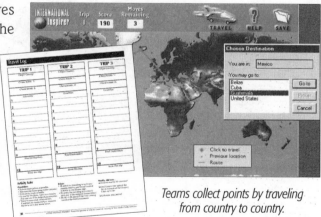

Teams collect points by traveling from country to country.

Of course, as with most small-group activities, the volume level in your classroom may rise a notch. Students will be arguing about whether to extend their path to Libya or leave themselves well-situated in Turkey for the next turn. They may be boisterously correcting each other. "Just because a country has a big population doesn't mean it's densely populated." Or you may hear them anxiously prodding their teammates for information. "Who has the map with sugar producers on it?" This kind of controlled chaos can be a little disconcerting, but once you hear the content of the conversations shooting around the classroom, it's tough to complain. After all, how often do you hear students talking excitedly about locational geography, world resource distribution, and international demographic patterns?

If you're new to this kind of group software experience, *International Inspirer* is a great place to start. The mix of collaboration within teams and competition for high scores between teams really gets everyone going. The computer manages the game, freeing you up to circulate among your students and seize upon any teachable moments you overhear. In addition, the software allows you to create your own categories and select starting locations, enabling you to align the experience more tightly with your curriculum. Students reinforce their content knowledge of locational geography with fun and repetition. In addition, they learn to work as a team, share resources, and listen to one another. Not a bad deal.

In order to make the computer lab more fun, I have started a competition among the students. Fifth-grade students use *National Inspirer* and sixth-grade students use *International Inspirer*. Students work in teams of two. Each team is given a set of maps or map books. The students then start the software and use their map skills as they travel to locations to earn points. The programs provide a wide variety of topics for each trip so the students are never researching the same thing. After they have completed all the trips required, they raise their hands and let me see their final score. If I do not see the score on the screen, their score does not count. (This usually only happens once!)

Each class's top scores for each level are displayed on the board in the lab for the other classes to see. Prizes are given at the end of the nine weeks to the top-scoring groups. Students love the competition, and teachers have found that this is a great program to help prepare for the Citizenship portion of the state proficiency test. The students don't even realize they are learning, and with a prize at the end, it's great fun!

Debbie Hunt
Miami East Intermediate
Casstown, Ohio

Memorable Drama

Narratives can have compelling power to convey content to students. A few years after leaving my classroom, students still remembered my lecture on "Mad-Dog" Decius. Okay, Decius, a respected Roman general and emperor, wasn't nicknamed "Mad-Dog" in real life, but in my story about how he rallied his troops in battle he certainly earned the moniker. The history I retold in that class, with a few admitted embellishments, had all the drama, tension, and excitement of a taut thriller. The students sat on the edges of their seats and later recalled the details I described better than I did. Drama has that kind of power.

Although history has a natural narrative flow to it, what about subjects like science and math? Sometimes a cross-curricular approach can help you embed core content into the personal dramas of inventors, scientists, and other thinkers. Stories of Archimedes of Syracuse from the 3rd century B.C. alone could entrance students, and help explain some of the fundamental principles of math and science. Images of Archimedes running naked through the streets of Sicily shouting, "Eureka!" or besting an enemy fleet with his creative war devices might provide much more memorable vehicles for students than reading a scientific definition of the theory of displacement or the workings of simple machines. The incredible resources that the computer and the Internet put at your fingertips can provide you access to these stories to integrate into your dazzling presentations.

But not all stories have to be history. Taking advantage of the rich multimedia world the computer offers allows us to create fictional, interactive dramas in which relevant content matters. Here's how it works: The computer presents a compelling situation demanding immediate action. Students have to decide what to do, and the information that guides their decisions contains curricular content. Learning the content is essential to move the story forward and find the correct solution. Like any good drama, students want to know what happens next. When the content is placed in a meaningful context, students are motivated to learn, and have fun doing it.

Let's take a peek at an example from a CD-ROM series called *Science Seekers,* which was developed by Tom Snyder Productions with support from NASA, the American Museum of Natural History, and top scientists from around the country. A fictional drama puts students in the role of troubleshooters who work at the Center for Science Seekers. When there's a problem that involves science, who should you call? Science Seekers, of course. One title in the series deals with a polluted aquifer. Another asks students to investigate a declining sea-otter population. The example we'll consider is based on an actual search for dinosaur fossils in the Gobi Desert. The real paleontologists and geologists used satellite imagery to help narrow down good places to look for fossils, and that's exactly what students do in *Science Seekers: Hidden in Rocks.* First, the whole class watches a short video that plays from the CD-ROM and presents the beginning of the story. A large new area, known as Vastland, has recently been opened to scientists, but the window for exploration is short because of a looming storm season. Paleontologists hope to uncover rich troves of fossils, but they need to narrow their search quickly. Unfortunately, the only available information on this secluded land consists of satellite data. The Science Seekers team is called in to review the data and images and recommend a search location from among six choices. And time is running out.

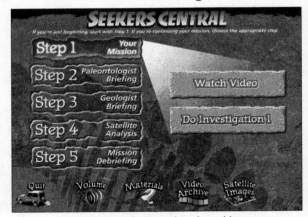

The first step is to watch a short video.

The drama captures students' attention, but they take responsibility for inserting the content rather than just having it told to them. Using a mixed-expert grouping method similar to *International Inspirer,* students work in teams with each team member responsible for complementary information. In order to evaluate the satellite data, students need to know how sedimentary, igneous, and meta-morphic rocks are formed, and which landforms might be associated with each one. Students also need to know how fossils are formed and uncovered. In what type of rock would scientists most likely find intact fossils from tens of millions of years ago? And what natural processes would help to uncover those fossils and make them easier to find?

The software comes with printed handouts that contain the content information students need to find the answers to these questions. Each member of a team has a different handout. In the first stage of the investigation, students focus on landforms. How does uplift change earth's surface and help make fossils easier to find?

One student learns about folding and faulting, another about volcanoes, a third about plate tectonics, and a fourth about earthquakes—all powerful forces that help shape the Earth's surface. Students share information as they answer a set of questions and review the satellite imagery. Students write down their group's answers to the questions on an Investigation sheet. Then the class comes together, and the software steps you through each question. It's a great opportunity for you to assess what students are learning, review answers, and reinforce the content for the whole class. At this point middle school science teacher Monica Hayes, who teaches in Decatur, Illinois, uses the program's Random Student Picker feature to call on students from different groups. She says it's a great mechanism to help make sure all students are pre-pared because, "You can't hide from the Random Student Picker. Teachers are likely to call on students in the 'T-zone' — in the front and down the center of the room. With the Random Student Picker, it's not in my hands anymore. Students can't hide, and they can't look away. They're all waiting on the edges of their seats."

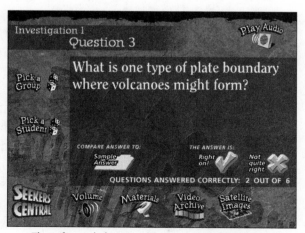

The software helps you review answers with students.

The investigation progresses through two more stages. In the second stage, students learn about sedimentary, igneous, and metamorphic rock formations, and the rock cycle, and apply that information to determine which type of rock is most likely to contain intact fossils. In the third stage, students learn about weathering, erosion, and layering of rock. With this last bit of knowledge, students have all the information they need to determine which of the six possible fossil sites is the most promising, and make their recommendation to the team of paleontologists and geologists in Vastland. If it's incorrect, the scientists will miss their opportunity for great fossil discoveries. If correct, the students can all cheer their new knowledge and their winning analysis. Students have fun, manipulate content in a memorable dramatic context, and reinforce all that other good stuff.

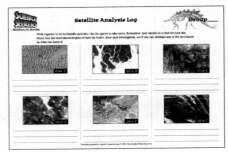

The technology can add fun, excitement, and drama to the content you're trying to convey. But you, the teacher, are the facilitator, and the technology is merely a tool in your hands.

From locational geography to history to science facts to the multiplication table, content forms a crucial part of our educational goals for our students. Technology can help support the teaching strategies you'll employ to achieve those goals. Not only does the software I've described help students learn important content, but it gives you, the teacher, opportunities to assess what students are learning and review the content with them. The technology can add fun, excitement, and drama to the content you're trying to convey. But you, the teacher, are the facilitator, and the technology is merely a tool in your hands.

Skill Mastery

Among our educational goals we require not just that students *know* but that they also *do.* In my category scheme, the doing part falls under the umbrella of skills — actions that are repeated in different contexts. In music the skills of reading music and playing notes correctly are repeated from song to song. In baseball, the skill of hitting a ball with a bat is repeated with different pitchers and different types of pitches. In math, the skill of division is repeated with different numbers. The multiplication table, on the other hand, always uses the same numbers, which is why I label it content rather than skill. That content knowledge is used when employing the skills of multiplication and division with bigger numbers. The skill of reading, particularly as it is being developed, also draws on content knowledge about letters and letter sounds. Once again I'll turn to standardized tests to highlight some concrete examples of the important skills we expect our students to master.

The 2001 Grade 6 Texas Assessment of Academic Skills evaluates student learning in mathematics and reading. Both subject areas are skill intensive, and the tests reflect this emphasis on skill. There are numerous questions that require students to solve word problems. Students must demonstrate their ability to identify the problem that needs to be solved, select the appropriate operations, and correctly perform the computation. Some questions require both content and skill. Take, for example, the question: What is the prime factorization of 54? Students must remember what the term *prime factorization* means, and then they must apply the appropriate skill to determine that it's 2×3^3. Some questions, such as the one below, demand that students interpret data presented in different formats, like a graph.

The Highland Middle School Spanish Club worked on several projects last year. The graph shows the number of hours spent on each project.

Which chart shows the same information that is shown on the graph?

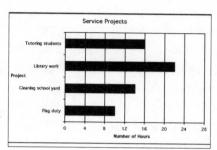

Service Projects

A

Project	Number of Hours
Tutoring students	16
Library work	20
Cleaning school yard	12
Flag duty	8

B

Project	Number of Hours
Tutoring students	8
Library work	11
Cleaning school yard	7
Flag duty	5

C

Project	Number of Hours
Tutoring students	10
Library work	14
Cleaning school yard	16
Flag duty	22

D

Project	Number of Hours
Tutoring students	16
Library work	22
Cleaning school yard	14
Flag duty	10

The Reading section of the test repeats the pattern. Students read a passage and then answer a series of multiple-choice questions. The questions ask students to infer meaning, summarize events, identify the main idea, and so on through a range of reading-comprehension skills.

The Florida and Massachusetts state tests go further. In math, both states include questions that are not multiple choice, requiring students not only to show the correct answer but also to explain how they solved the problem. The ability to put mathematical operations into language involves valuable higher-order skills that cannot be machine scored. Someone has to read and evaluate the quality of those responses. In reading, too, both the Florida and Massachusetts tests require open-ended responses from students. Test-takers read passages, answer multiple-choice questions, and write short essays using examples from the reading. Social studies and science tests, in the states that have them, also assess writing skills along with domain-specific skills, such as map-reading and data analysis.

The skills that we want our students to develop and that are assessed on state tests cannot be memorized. The type of direct instruction that can work well with content won't do the trick when your goal for students is skill mastery. Facility with a skill comes with mentoring and practice. A teacher demonstrates a skill and the learner, through repeated iterations, grasps it and then hones it. Worksheets provide one of the most common and straightforward ways to reinforce a skill that a teacher has modeled for the class. The various worksheet- and puzzle-generating programs I described earlier can be tailored to the specific math or language skills you want students to practice. There are also many software programs designed for student use that can help reinforce a narrow set of skills in a one-on-one setting. Some programs even allow you to customize the skills students practice, and will track their performance.

Practicing Math Word Problem Skills

Try this problem from an NAEP mathematics test:

> Sam can purchase his lunch at school. Each day he wants to have juice that costs 50¢, a sandwich that costs 90¢, and fruit that costs 35¢. His mother has only $1.00 bills. What is the least number of $1.00 bills that his mother should give him so he will have enough money to buy lunch for 5 days?[28]

Did you come up with the answer "9 dollar bills"? If you didn't, don't feel badly; only 17% of 8th graders scored a correct response on this problem. But a good number of students who got the question wrong got the math right! It's not that complicated. 50¢ + 90¢ + 35¢ = $1.75 per day. $1.75 * 5 = $8.75 a week.

And $8.75 is the answer many students gave to the problem. They got the computation right. Unfortunately, they got the question wrong.

For many kids, computation is not the problem. But plug those numbers into a sentence about a train traveling west at 45 mph and suddenly, they're lost. Try presenting the problem below to a group of students. (The question is a variation of another NAEP problem.)

A shepherd manages a flock of 25 sheep. He spends 10 hours a day with the sheep. The fields where he tends the sheep are 4 miles from the shepherd's home, where he lives with his family of 5. How old is the shepherd?

Of course, there's no way you can figure the age of the shepherd from the information above, but that won't stop many computation-happy kids from offering answers like 29, 35, or 30. Give students some numbers and they feel compelled to manipulate them — add them, subtract them, multiply, or divide, even if they don't know what the question is.

If we want students to score better on tests, if we want them to be able to handle problems in context, we need to teach them to identify the question first before leaping into computing the answer. As the father in Avi's children's book, *No More Magic,* constantly reminds his son: "Get the questions right before you get the answers wrong." The character in the book is talking about life, not math, and of course we hope that (in both areas) students will get the answers right too. Certainly, we need to teach students math facts. They need to be able to use the basic operations, manage fractions and percents, handle measurements and decimals. These are basic skills, critical to our children's success in the world. What's missing is another critical basic skill — knowing when to use which operation. If we can teach students to get the questions right, we can greatly increase their chances of getting the answers right too.

There are lots of math programs on the market designed to help students practice their computation skills but few that address the kinds of difficulties students increasingly encounter on state and national tests. In many states students take math tests as early as 4th grade that measure their ability not just to solve word problems but to explain the solution process. They must be able to identify the question that needs to be answered, pick out the relevant information, perform the computations, and then describe how they did it. That's a tall order that can't be filled by simply memorizing math facts or practicing computation skills.

If we can teach students to get the questions right, we can greatly increase their chances of getting the answers right too.

Math Mysteries is a CD-ROM series by Tom Snyder Productions that targets the basic skills necessary for solving the types of word problems found on these tests. Each of the five titles in the *Math Mysteries* series is designed to help teachers model how to attack different types of word problems. The program uses animated characters to present specific problems

Animated characters present problems to the students.

that highlight different problem-solving techniques. Then, guided by the teacher and working in cooperative groups, students learn to identify the right question, pick out the important information, and set up a solution plan.

Once the teacher has modeled this process with the class, her students can practice and hone these skills independently. In addition to a whole-class CD-ROM, each *Math Mysteries* title includes another CD filled with word problems for individual student practice. Students can explore a 3-D environment where they'll meet interesting characters, solve math problems, and gather clues to solve a bigger mystery. A built-in "MathPad" helps students organize the information they gather, set up a plan to attack the problem, perform computations, and submit answers. As they work, the software captures student performance so that

you can review their progress. Mary Brown, who teaches 6th-grade math in San Diego, says that even some of her brightest students have a hard time with word problems. "*Math Mysteries* shows students the step-by-step logical thinking that they're going to have to go through when they do algebra and more complicated mathematics."

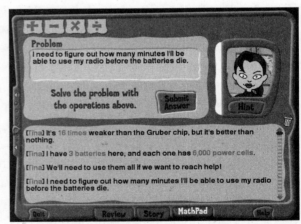

Students use a MathPad to collect information.

Practicing Reading Comprehension Skills

Reading for Meaning is another software program that offers both a teacher-led modeling component for use with a whole class, and a student practice component.

With *Reading for Meaning,* teachers can introduce and reinforce core reading-comprehension skills including main idea, inference, sequence, compare and contrast, and cause and effect. In the teacher-led modeling lesson on main idea, for instance, students watch a short animation on the computer about a group of kids at the beach having a conversation. The topic of their conversation? Not surprisingly, it's the beach. But what's the main idea? Step-by-step, the teacher leads students through the process of identifying the main idea and supporting details, and completing an online graphic organizer.

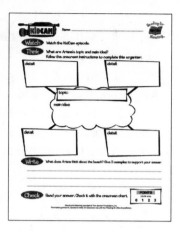

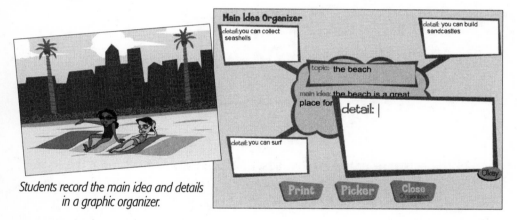

Students record the main idea and details in a graphic organizer.

In the next step of the program, students respond to a question about the story they just watched, similar to the types of questions asked on many states' standardized tests. On their worksheets, students summarize the main idea, supporting their answers with examples from the story. In the final step, students are asked to review and score their answer based on a simple rubric. The program gives students practice with the rubric by supplying sample responses of varying quality for students to score. This helps the teacher lead a class discussion on what makes one answer good, and another not so good. Students then score their own responses.

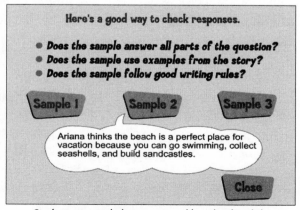

Students assess their responses with a simple rubric.

Completing this modeling lesson prepares students for subsequent lessons where they are asked to find the main idea in a reading passage. The software provides practice lessons with authentic literature crossing genres and ability levels. Students read a passage, work in groups to complete a graphic organizer, and then respond independently to three short-answer questions about the reading. Each skill covered in the program follows the same pattern, employing an appropriate graphic organizer. The software captures student work so the teacher can review progress. The tools and process are easily adaptable to the teacher's specific reading selections. And the group work that is part of the modeling phases of both *Math Mysteries* and *Reading for Meaning* enables you to incorporate cooperative learning and teamwork while building essential, core skills in math and language arts.

Computer software can be very good at capturing and reporting results. But diagnosing the cause of mistakes and perceiving areas that need improvement often require direct student observation.

Both of the software programs I've described help students develop basic skills. Although students can use them independently, the programs include whole-class components. Practicing these skills in public, or at least in front of a teacher adds a level of diagnostic insight that solitary computer practice can't quite achieve. Take my son's saxophone playing…again. (Hey, I hear it every night so it's on my mind.) At his lesson, his music teacher might model a new song that requires some tricky fingering. All week my son practices what he has learned. Now, imagine that instead of returning in person for his next lesson, my son simply sent a tape recording of his best rendition of the new song to his teacher. The sound of the music on the tape would tell the instructor whether or not my son can play the song correctly, but it won't necessarily tell the teacher how his student can get better. For that kind of insight, the music teacher needs to observe the skill in use; he needs to see my son's breathing and fingering, maybe even his toe-tapping and posture. He needs to hear where my son hesitates, and where he gets notes confused. Then he can suggest specific changes that will lead to improvement. The same holds true for skills developed in school. Computer software can be very good at capturing and reporting results. But diagnosing the cause of mistakes and perceiving areas that need improvement often require direct student observation. Integrating whole-class and small-group practice opportunities provides you with a glimpse of your students' skills in use, helping you identify the best intervention strategies for them.

Concept Understanding

Deep understanding. Who could argue with that educational goal? But what exactly is it? Content and skills, what we expect students to remember and do, can be readily identified in state curriculum frameworks and tests. The "other good stuff" and conceptual understanding aren't so easy to define and measure. To return to my earlier analogies of baseball and music, it's a deep understanding of the game that enables a baseball player to create strategy and to anticipate what will happen next. A similar level of understanding in my saxophone-playing son will empower him not just to play the instrument correctly, but to someday generate new tunes, putting notes together in new and interesting ways. In school, conceptual understanding is reflected in students who exceed the mechanics of writing, who act like scientists, who think like mathematicians, and who see connections among events today and in the past. Some simple examples will hopefully illuminate the distinctiveness of my definition of conceptual understanding.

Let's start with something simple like number sense. Children start by memorizing numbers and counting from one to ten. There are, however, a lot of numbers, an infinite number of numbers, in fact, simple and complex. Children simply can't memorize them all. They need an understanding of numbers, a number sense, if you will, that empowers them to recognize that a half of something is less than a whole of that thing or that 1/16 is larger than .000735. We can teach students the algorithm for comparing numbers and expect them to practice it when confronted with a new, unfamiliar pair of values. But when they understand numbers, they will have less need for so formulaic an approach. They will picture what those numbers mean. They'll even be able to generate and envision their own numbers and how they relate.

In science or social studies, students without conceptual understanding will similarly get stuck when they need to generate new ideas or explanations for phenomena they have not previously studied. Students can memorize, for instance, the definition of the water cycle in the same way they can learn the three main causes of the Civil War. But only students who understand the water cycle might accurately predict on what mornings the dew on the ground will be thick or devise a creative plan to defog the bathroom mirror. And only those who understand patterns in history will see the connections between the forces that led to civil war in the United States and the economic and social forces that lead to internal violence in many parts of the world today.

Conceptual understanding is reflected in students who exceed the mechanics of writing, who act like scientists, who think like mathematicians, and who see connections among events today and in the past.

In language arts, readers who understand theme and symbolism will have deep insight into what they read, exceeding the literal words of the passage. With an understanding of how an author crafts the style of his or her writing with purpose and audience, students can greatly enhance both their reading and writing. Student writers with the kind of understanding I'm describing can move past the defined structure of topic sentence, body text, and concluding sentence. Those without that understanding are stuck plugging sentences into a rigid format like numbers into an equation.

Developing Concepts Through Conversation

Building students' conceptual understanding demands an instructional method different from that which you might select for content acquisition or skill mastery. Lectures and slide-show presentations might be a good way to introduce a concept to students. But as a teacher I found that when students explain what they have learned, when they really use it, they then own it. The deepest understanding came when they articulated their thoughts to others, especially fellow students. Lev Vygotsky, the noted Russian psychologist, was a key figure in the study of the relationship between language and learning in the 20th century. Vygotsky followed and admired the work of Jean Piaget, who concentrated on the cognitive development of children. Piaget was fascinated by what went on inside the heads of youngsters and saw language as the result of that cognitive activity. Vygotsky, on the other hand, saw language as a driver of cognitive development. To illustrate his point, Vygotsky compared language usage to drawing among young children. Ask a very young child what she is drawing, and you're likely to get a blank look. The child needs to finish the drawing, step back to look at it, and then she can tell you what it is. The act of drawing defines the child's intent. Language, Vygotsky argued, works much the same way. The act of putting thought into words actually helps define the thought.

Think back to your first years of teaching — when the material you had to cover may have been somewhat new to you — and you'll likely recognize what Vygotsky was talking about. For me the difference between learning as a student and learning as a teacher was extreme. As a student I learned mainly for myself. When I did share information, it was usually with the teacher, who already knew it. As a teacher, on the other hand, I was responsible for conveying concepts, content, and skills that were new to my audience. I had to think about how others would understand the material. The act of creating that explanation, of putting the content into my own words, increased my own understanding. The same is true for students when they're put in situations that require them to explain concepts to one another. Jim Patton, who teaches at the Hillcrest Professional Development School in Waco, Texas, uses this technique in his classroom. He says, "In a way, communication is like teaching. When students have to communicate to other students how they came to an answer or solution, it reinforces their own

The deepest understanding came when they articulated their thoughts to others, especially fellow students.

understanding of how they came to that solution." When students are creating a shared language for a common meaning, whether it's in the form of words, pictures, or physical objects, they are developing deep conceptual understandings.

Developing Science Concepts

Concept-building conversations among students are the basis of a CD-ROM series called *Science Court* by Tom Snyder Productions. Based on the animated series with the same name on ABC-TV, the program combines the fun animated stories from the television show with hands-on experiences and classroom conversation to help kids understand difficult science concepts.

Like the *Decisions, Decisions* series described earlier, *Science Court* calls for students to work in groups of four. Each student in a group gets a slightly different worksheet. They all have the same set of six questions to answer, but each student has different information to help answer those questions. After watching part of a story on CD-ROM, students are left with a cliffhanger. In one title, *Science Court: Water Cycle,* for instance, Pip Peterson is accused of making leaky pipes, which caused I. M. Richman to slip and fall in the subway. During the trial the prosecuting attorney, the bumbling but lovable Doug Savage, tries to prove his case by arguing that the moisture on the outside of a glass of ice water came from inside the glass, just like the water dripping from Pip Peterson's pipes. Is he right?

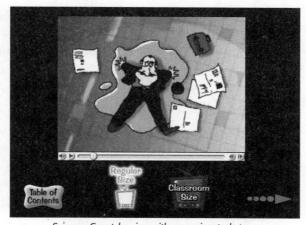

Science Court *begins with an animated story.*

The video stops, and students turn to their worksheets to answer six questions. Students go to work in their groups. They talk to each other, sharing the different information on their worksheets and trying out a hands-on activity (which in this case involves condensing water on the outside of an empty cold glass). As they work through the questions they must answer, students begin to build a shared understanding of the water cycle. The story helps them build that understanding by giving them a context in which they can apply their knowledge to a real-life situation — dripping pipes.

When they've answered all the questions in their group, students turn back to the CD-ROM. The program asks each question one at a time. The teacher can use a built-in random student picker to select who should answer. Students turn their worksheets over so that they can't look at their group's answers. That means each student really needs to know each answer. The class as a whole must answer at least four of the six questions correctly, or they have to start over. If they get enough right, they predict what will happen in the trial and watch the results.

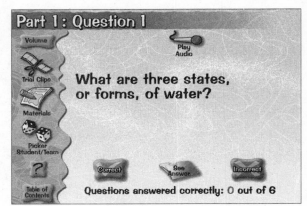

Students respond to six questions.

Using this method, *Science Court* encourages both group and individual student accountability. Students in a group are under positive pressure to coach each other to a level of unsupported understanding. They can't just copy the answers, especially for the questions that require explanations and original thinking. If everyone in the group isn't adequately prepared, the whole class suffers. The conversations that result from this positive peer pressure are meaningful and wonderful to hear.

Developing Math Concepts

Math is another area in which conceptual understanding is crucial for long-term success. Unfortunately, as I learned from personal experience, conceptual understanding of math is often overshadowed by computation. I was a straight-A student in math from elementary school right through high school. I was the odds-on favorite in any flashcard competition, and everyone wanted to be my partner for group work. I remember my 5th-grade teacher regularly urging me to show my work. I never did, and she had to concede, "You can't argue with success." And success in K–12 math, whether it was simple multiplication and division or advanced trigonometry, meant getting the correct answer.

Math is another area in which conceptual understanding is crucial for long-term success.

Riding this history of right answers, I entered upper-level calculus as a freshman at Yale brimming with confidence. I had scored well on my Advanced Placement exams, and I figured math in college would continue to be easy. Wrong! I was completely lost. Suddenly, math wasn't just about right answers. Being able to complete volumes of computations wasn't enough. I had to know what I was doing, and I had to be able to articulate it. There was a large gap in my math education, one that needn't have waited until college to be filled. In fact, it should have been addressed early on. It's great when students can fill in rows of answers on a math worksheet; it's even better when they grasp the concepts behind the computation and can describe how they got those answers.

Fizz & Martina's Math Adventures is a series of math CD-ROMs from Tom Snyder Productions that attempts to fill this gap, requiring elementary students to articulate the process of math problem solving. First, the teacher divides the class into small groups. With the computer connected to a large monitor, the teacher invites students to gather around. The software leads the teacher through the distribution of follow-along worksheets and the assignment of a color to each team. Unlike the complementary information approach used in programs like *Science Court* and *International Inspirer,* this program requires that each team member have exactly the same print materials in hand.

The CD-ROM and worksheets operate in conjunction with one another. The software tells students to get their pencils poised for taking notes. Then a video story unfolds, filling the computer monitor so that it resembles watching TV. If you're viewing *Blue Falls Elementary,* a title in the series that deals with multistep addition and multiplication, you'll see the characters gather for a special club meeting. The first order of business is Martina's late dues. The club desperately

needs the money to continue work on Project Sphinx. Martina is three weeks late paying her dues. Students jot some notes on their worksheets. Dues are six dollars a week (more notes). Martina worries whether she has enough money to pay what she owes. She has only twenty dollars (one final jot). Will she have to run home to get more money?

The animated story puts math problems in a real-life context.

The video stops. You can see that, as in real life, there's a lot happening. Students are captured by the rich drama, and they have a genuine problem to solve. One

teacher in California said her students were so eager to solve the problem that they'd start talking as soon as they thought they heard a clue in the video. She had to remind her students to wait until the video stopped or they might miss something. In their groups students sift through the information and set to work. The worksheet for this episode asks three questions. First, "How much does Martina owe the club?" Calculating this answer isn't usually the toughest challenge for the group, assuming they have all the correct information (and among the team members they almost always do).

It's the second question that provides the most significant challenge for students, and not surprisingly, it's the question that builds the most understanding of what they have just done. "Write, in a complete sentence (or two), how you figured out the answer to question 1. Do NOT use numbers in your explanation." The computation is trivial compared to the task of articulating that mathematical process, of explaining what they did. "Well, I multiplied one week's dues by the number of weeks Martina was behind..." With this step, math becomes something more than mere number manipulation. It has to do with real life and concrete processes. Making this leap is an incredible effort for kids, but it is a worthwhile one. And they get better and better with practice.

The third question asks students to explain why the answer to the problem is important for Martina. The final step demands that the group return to the original context. In life, the story doesn't end with the numerical answer. The response to a problem has consequences. In this case, Martina doesn't have to run home. As in life, the drama continues.

Once students have completed the three questions, the teacher can use the software's built-in Group Picker feature to select one of the groups. The teacher can then ask an individual student in that group to answer the first question. When I've done this with students, I'll pick up a student's worksheet so that he or she must answer the question not through memorization, but through understanding. If the student's response is correct, both orally and on the worksheet, everyone on the team gets an award card that depicts one of the characters from the video. (You can give these award cards any value you want, but don't worry, the students will give them more worth than you could ever assign.) If the student gets the answer wrong, no one on the team gets an award card. It's a standard cooperative learning technique used to diffuse responsibility. The important role for the teacher is to constantly reinforce the group over the individual. So when one team member is incorrect, it is not the single student who failed the group, it is the group that failed the student. I'll say to the student, "Too bad your teammates let you down. I'm sure they won't let it happen again." It's amazing how quickly a group will then work to embrace its struggling members.

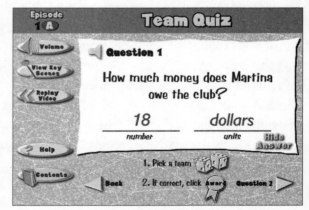

The teacher reviews the correct answers with students.

Teacher Tip

Learning to think mathematically is so important for students. *Fizz and Martina* helps children develop their math thinking skills because they have to express their thinking to other children. The first time I used *Fizz and Martina*, I took the program home and previewed it ahead of time. I read the teacher's guide, and I felt familiar with it, but I was still a little nervous because reading the teacher's guide doesn't guarantee that it's going to go perfectly in class. Even on my first try it was quite successful. Now, after two or three years, I've refined the process a bit. I'll use the program three days in a row, and then take two days off to reinforce arithmetic skills or do other math-related activities. Then I'll come back to it again. With this method, one program ends up being about 9 sessions. The students look forward to it and it helps me meet my goals to get students talking mathematically and communicating their ideas to each other.

Beth Thieman
3rd- & 4th-grade teacher
Buckingham, Browne & Nichols School
Cambridge, Massachusetts

As the teacher works through the problem with students, the CD-ROM keeps track of the activity and offers sample correct responses for students to compare to their own. When the video continues, the answers are immediately integrated into the story and new problems emerge. The video sets the scene, builds the drama, and controls the pacing. Supported by the computer, you run the activity with the class, and with the help of some simple cooperative learning strategies, it's a dynamic one.

Developing Graphing Concepts

The area of graphing requires an intersection of content knowledge, skills, and conceptual understanding. Students must develop the skill of extracting data from a graph. They must remember graphing terminology, like *x-axis, y-axis,* and *median.* But for students to be savvy consumers of graphic information, they must develop a deeper conceptual understanding of the information a graph can display and how that information can be used.

Let's say you're trying to teach students the concept of mean or average. You might ask students to figure the average age of three people aged 10, 11, and 15. Teaching the formula for finding an average, you'd have students add the three ages ($10+11+15=36$) and divide by the total number of people ($36\div3=12$). The average, or mean, is 12. Now, a teacher friend of mine recently told me about one of her students who claimed, "I calculated the mean, and it's bigger than any of the data." The student didn't express any concern or wonder with his result. He just stated it. Of course, that situation — the average being larger than any of the data — is impossible. Clearly, the student made a mistake in his calculations. But without a conceptual understanding of what an average is, he couldn't see that his result was not just incorrect but impossible.

Graphing software can help reinforce concepts and give students a way to visualize abstract ideas like average. *Graph Master* by Tom Snyder Productions is a data analysis and graphing tool that is designed not just to make graphs but to actual-

ly help teach graphing. Using a tool like *Graph Master,* you could demonstrate for students how to create a line plot of the ages you want to average.

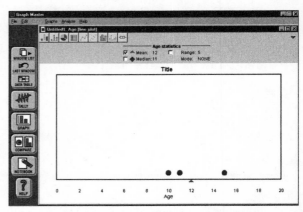

Graph Master highlights the mean on the graph. With this graph, you might push your students' concept of average by asking them to add two more people to the mix, but keep the average age at 12. As students experiment with a tool like this, concepts like mean, median, and mode will become much clearer. The program includes specific directed tasks to highlight these concepts that you can do with your class, or assign individually to students who need more practice.

You can display mean, median, mode, and range.

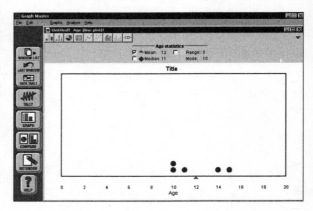

In addition to using *Graph Master* to illuminate concepts like mean, median, and mode, the program can also help students understand how to read graphs as well. Those who know how to use graphs can greatly influence our perception of the information they convey. Look, for instance, at the two graphs showing student test scores in five fictitious towns. Publish the graph

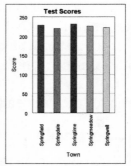

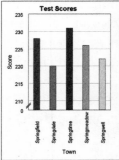

on the right in the newspaper, and the property values in Springdale could drop 10 percent, even though the only difference in the two graphs is a change in the scale. *Graph Master* gives students an opportunity to play with the scales and observe data displayed in different ways.

Developing Geography Concepts

Another area where a visual tool can help students develop concepts is geography. Interpreting maps is a challenge for many students, and they need lots of practice to be able to make the conceptual leap from the real world to a 2-dimensional representation of the world on a map. *Neighborhood MapMachine* by Tom Snyder Productions is a program you and your students can use to make and then explore neighborhood maps. You can begin by choosing a size for your map, and then laying down roads, and adding houses, stores, and other buildings. You can also add other symbols such as cars, traffic lights, and people to the map. Finally, you can add physical features, like parks, lakes, and trees.

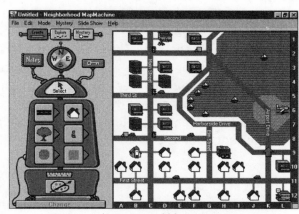

In Create mode you can add features to your map.

At this point, you can print your map on one or more pages to hand out to students or display in your classroom. But you can also give students a chance to explore the map on the computer. For example, let's say you want to give students practice using the map scale to estimate distance. You could add a note to your map challenging students to predict the distance from, say, the police station to the airport. In Explore mode, students can use the ruler feature to measure the distance on the map in inches. Then, they can use the map scale to figure the distance, and type in their prediction. Finally, they can use the compass to navigate the map, tracking the actual distance as they move a marker around the map.

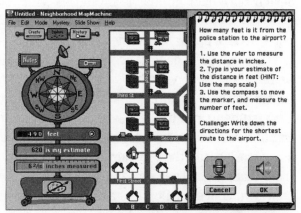

In Explore mode students can use the map to measure distances.

Teacher Tip

In our 7th-grade foreign language class we teach both French and Spanish. We are always looking for ways to use technology in our class. We planned on using *Neighborhood MapMachine* to teach directions and building names that could be found in a typical French-speaking or Spanish-speaking town. We had no idea the impact it would have on our students!

First, we taught students the basic words for getting around in a foreign city and the names of typical buildings that a traveler would encounter. Using the software, the Spanish teacher and I made a city. We labeled the streets and buildings in both French and Spanish. We then used the built-in recording device to create a scavenger hunt in the city. Each building was either French-speaking or Spanish-speaking. The students were then set free to gather items, follow clues, follow directions, and of course to learn some new French and Spanish vocabulary. They were directed to building after building in the city. The kids loved hearing their teachers' voices coming out of the computer. We even named some of the houses after the kids in the class, which was a fun addition. It was marvelous to hear the kids actually speaking French and Spanish as they repeated the directions and clues. By the end, they all wanted to make their own maps — *en français et español*! This made the learning of simple directions and buildings in French and Spanish a real experience for the kids.

Jim Ward & Cathy Sylvester
Brittany Hill Middle School
Blue Springs, Missouri

As children create maps and then navigate them, they develop important conceptual understandings of map symbols, direction, scale, grid coordinates, and other geography skills. You can even use *Neighborhood MapMachine* to design scavenger hunt-style mysteries with your maps for students to solve.

The software programs I've described in this section are powerful resources that can help you build deep concept understanding in your students. Visual tools like *Graph Master* and *Neighborhood MapMachine* can serve both as an explanatory aid for you and as an exploratory environment for your students. With guided tasks, students can begin to take ownership of the concepts you introduce. Both *Fizz and Martina's Math Adventures* and *Science Court* are centered around dramatic stories, and the programs are designed with an infrastructure for fostering shared language. They demand that students explain to each other to reinforce their own conceptual understanding. With these resources you, the teacher, can help your students build solid understandings of difficult concepts. The power of that effort can last a lifetime.

Conclusion

Good teachers are always thinking about how they can make their classrooms a little better. When they try something new, they're always thinking about how to refine it, experiment with it, revise it, or try a different angle. They're always thinking about how they can make learning more meaningful to students and how to get students actively involved in learning. I think of computers as a tool to help them achieve this goal.

Richard Bruno
7th-Grade Math/Science Teacher
Jack Benny Middle School
Waukegan, Illinois

Conclusion

Educational technology, from silent films to interactive multimedia, has promised in its multiple incarnations nothing short of a complete reinvention of teaching and learning. In some cases, the most ardent technology advocates predicted not just the replacement of teachers but the complete dissolution of schools as institutions. Most of these expectations were doomed from the outset, and, as Larry Cuban pointed out in his 1986 book *Teachers and Machines,* teachers typically bore the burden of blame for each failure. Cuban noted a period of "teacher bashing" that followed each set of failed expectations.[29]

The teacher bashing continues today as technology reformers scratch their heads over the limited impact that computers have had on teaching practice. Despite the incredible amount of money spent on technology, not much seems to have changed. The way schools and classrooms work today is remarkably similar to the way they worked before they were loaded up with wires and machines. Teachers are accused of resisting change, of being afraid of the technology, and of being computer illiterate.

We have seen, however, that teachers do embrace technology. The chalkboard, the filmstrip, and the overhead projector were all, at one point, innovative devices; each became a powerful and regularly used instructional tool in teachers' hands. And the charge that today's teachers are technophobes fails to hold up under scrutiny. Larry Cuban's more recent study of computers in classrooms found that "Students and teachers showed little evidence of technophobia or resistance to using information technologies."[30] Indeed, he found that teachers were avid users of computers at home.

The disconnect comes when we look at computer use in the classroom. I find that when I ask a teacher if he or she uses a computer, I often receive a guilty negative shake of the head. When I probe further, though, I get a different response. "Do you e-mail parents?" Yes. "Do you search the Web for lesson ideas and content information?" Absolutely. "Do you use a word processor, database, or electronic gradebook?" Yes, yes, and sometimes. "What do you mean, then, when you say you don't use the computer?" Well, I don't use it for teaching. The final admission is typically accompanied by downcast eyes and a guilty tone. These teachers want to make technology work in their classrooms. Yet despite their best efforts, it doesn't always fit in.

My associate of many years, Tom Snyder, has illuminated the relationship between schools and technology with a medical analogy: A patient has been informed by his doctors that his heart is failing. Without a transplant, he'll very likely die. Fortunately, some well-meaning technicians have developed a new, artificial heart that has performed superbly in lab testing. In the face of such a dire diagnosis, the patient accepts the artificial transplant. The surgeons perform the operation and hopes are high for a complete recovery. But the heart soon begins to falter. The technicians check their device. It's working as it should. They start yelling at the patient. "What's wrong with you?! What are you doing with our wonderful heart?" The patient responds that he's trying to make it work. He wants to live and to thrive, but his body keeps trying to reject the artificial device. Nothing the technicians or the patient do seems to help. Finally, frustrated and angry, the doctors remove the artificial heart and put back the old one, which, despite all the dire predictions, just keeps on beating.

So it has been with some of the technologies that have been implanted in our schools. No matter how hard teachers and administrators try, some devices never become part of the living organism of the school. What will be the fate of the computer and the other interactive technologies it has spawned? If software developers, technology advocates, and the general public continue in the belief that computer technology will one day replace teachers and make schools obsolete, I predict they will be disappointed. However, if we design the technology to conform to the pulse and nature of the school, if we build it to fit in rather than to reconfigure, then it may yet be embraced by teachers. If we can help teachers harness the power of today's technology as a tool to enhance and support their efforts, computers can make a positive difference in the quality of teaching and learning.

Notes

1. The National Commission on Excellence in Education, *A Nation at Risk: The Imperative for Educational Reform, A Report to the Nation and the Secretary of Education, United States Department of Education,* April, 1983.

2. Lowell C. Rose and Alec M. Gallup, "The 33rd Annual Phi Delta Kappa/Gallup Poll of the Public's Attitudes Toward the Public Schools," September, 2001.

3. "The Moving Picture and the National Character," in *The American Review of Reviews* (September, 1910), p. 317, and Pierce J. Fleming, "Moving Pictures as a Factor in Education," in *The Pedagogical Seminary* (September, 1911), p. 342.

4. William Inglis, "Edison and the New Education," *Harper's Weekly* (November 4, 1911), p. 7.

5. J. W. Shepherd, "The Teaching Efficiency of the Film," *The Educational Screen* (June, 1922), p. 179.

6. Dudley Grant Hays, "Visual Education: Its Scope, Purpose and Value," *The Educational Screen* (February, 1923), p. 59.

7. Margaret Harrison, *Radio in the Classroom* (New York: Prentice-Hall, Inc., 1937), p. 4.

8. "Teaching by Television" (New York: Ford Foundation, 1961), pp. 7–10.

9. The ad was reproduced in Anthony G. Oettinger, "Run, Computer, Run." *The Mythology of Educational Innovation* (Cambridge, MA: Harvard University Press, 1969), p. 119.

10. Seymour Papert, *Mindstorms* (New York: Basic Books, 1980), p. 9.

11. For an excellent review of the history of educational film, radio, and TV, along with some great insight about integrating technology into the classroom, read Larry Cuban, *Teachers and Machines: The Classroom Use of Technology Since 1920* (New York: Teachers College Press, 1986). Another interesting read in this field is Philip Jackson, *The Teacher and the Machine* (Pittsburgh: University of Pittsburgh Press, 1968).

12. Major E. D. Mansfield, "The Military Academy at West Point," in *The American Journal of Education,* Henry Barnard, ed., vol. 13 (1863), pp. 31–33.

13. The reminiscences of Rev. Samuel J. May in *The American Journal of Education,* vol. 16 (1866), p. 142.

14. Henry Barnard, *First Annual Report to the School Commissioners of Connecticut, 1839,* as quoted in *A Cyclopedia of Education,* Paul Monroe, ed. (New York: The MacMillan Company, 1911), p. 391.

15. William A. Alcott, "Slate and Black Board Exercises for Common Schools" reprinted in *Connecticut Common School Journal,* vol. 4, nos. 8–11 (April 1, 1842 – May 15, 1842), p. 69.

16. Josiah Bumstead, "The Blackboard in the Primary School," in *Connecticut Common School Journal,* Vol. 4, no. 3; January 15, 1842.

17. Some good examples of these critics and academics include: Larry Cuban, *Oversold and Underused: Computers in Classrooms,* 1980–2000 (Cambridge, MA: Harvard University Press, 2001); Jane Healy, *Failure to Connect,* (Touchstone Books, 1999); and Todd Oppenheimer, "The Computer Delusion," in *The Atlantic Monthly,* July 1997.

18. "New Teaching Materials," in *The School Review* (November, 1946), p. 505.

19. "New Teaching Materials," p. 504.

20. "Technology Counts 2001: The New Divides," *Education Week,* May 10, 2001.

21. Larry Cuban, *Oversold and Underused: Computers in the Classroom* (Cambridge, Massachusetts: Harvard University Press, 2001), p. 133.

22. U.S. Department of Education, *A Talented, Dedicated, and Well-Prepared Teacher in Every Classroom* (September, 1999).

23. National Education Association, *Status of the American Public School Teacher 1995–96,* (July, 1997).

24. "Technology Counts '99: Building the Digital Curriculum," in *Education Week,* September, 1999.

25. As reported in the *Harvard Education Letter,* July/August 1997.

26. Susan Moore Johnson, et al., "The Project on the Next Generation of Teachers at the Harvard Graduate School of Education."

27. National Association of Colleges and Employers, *Job Outlook 2001.*

28. National Assessment of Educational Progress, Mathematics exam, 1996.

29. Larry Cuban, *Teachers and Machines: The Classroom Use of Technology since 1920* (New York: Teachers College Press, 1986).

30. Larry Cuban, *Oversold and Underused: Computers in the Classroom* (Cambridge, Massachusetts: Harvard University Press, 2001), p. 132.

Reference

Contents

Creating a Gradebook with *Excel*

Using Microsoft *Excel,* you can create a customized spreadsheet gradebook to help you record and average your students' grades. The following walkthrough is reprinted from the book *Excel Workshop for Teachers* by Janet Caughlin. In addition to step-by-step instructions for creating spreadsheets, charts, and graphs with *Excel*, the book includes tips and advice from classroom teachers as well as a CD-ROM packed with clip art, templates, and sample files.

Making a Template

Create a Gradebook

Don't waste your valuable time averaging grades! You can record your grades in a worksheet that will instantly average them for you. You'll make a simple gradebook in this exercise that you'll also be able to share with colleagues. More advanced gradebooks are found later in this chapter.

This Activity Covers the Following Topics
- Creating the Framework
- Using AutoFill
- Entering Formulas
- Formatting Cells
- Inserting a Header
- Filling Cells with Color
- Freezing Panes
- Protecting Cells
- Removing the Column and Row Headers
- Password-Protecting the File
- Opening a Password-Protected File

Creating the Framework

1. Create a new Worksheet document.

2. Click the **Select All** indicator to select all cells in the worksheet.

3. Click the **Format** menu and choose **Column**, then **Width**. Type "**4**" and click **OK**.

4. Click cell **A1** to remove the highlighting. Move the **mouse pointer** so it **rests on the line between the Column A and Column B Headers**. The cursor changes to a crosshair.

5. **Drag the crosshair to the right** until **Column A is three times as wide as it was**. See the screenshot on the top of the next page.

6. Using this method, make **Column B half again as wide as it was**.

7. Using this method, **make Row 1 twice as tall as it was**.

8. Click the **Row 1 Indicator**. Click the **Format** menu and choose **Cells**. Click the **Alignment** tab, then **Wrap text.** This lets text wrap inside a cell instead of moving to an adjacent cell. Click **OK**.

9. Click the **Column A Indicator**. Click the **Boldface** button or press **CTRL B** (Windows) **⌘ B** (Macintosh) to boldface the text.

10. Click the **Row 1 Indicator** and **boldface** the text in those cells.

Using AutoFill

1. Click cell **A1** and type "**Student.**" Press **TAB**. Type "**Average**" and press **TAB**.

2. Assignment titles will be entered in the remaining cells in Row 1. Click cell **C1** and type "**1.**" Press **TAB**. Click cell **D1** and type "**2.**"

3. **Select cells C1–D1**. Place the cursor on the **dot in the lower right corner of cell D1**. When it changes to match the screenshot, **drag right** to select the cells visible on the screen. When you release the mouse button, the cells will be filled.

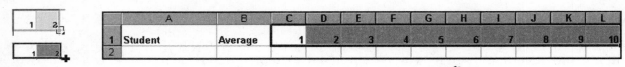

	A	B	C	D	E	F	G	H	I	J	K	L
1	Student	Average	1	2	3	4	5	6	7	8	9	10
2												

If you are entering daily grades, you could enter a date, then AutoFill will add a day to the date in each cell.

Entering Formulas

2001 only

1. Click cell **B3**, then click the **arrow next to the AutoSum** icon and drag to **Average** from the menu that appears. Skip to **Step 3 below**.

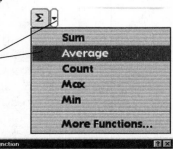

2000, 98, & 97

1. Click cell **B3** and click the **Paste Function** button.

2. Under **Function Category**, click **Statistical** and then under **Function Name**, click **Average**. Click **OK**. A dialog box appears. Drag it down and out of the way.

3. Select cell **C3 and all visible cells in Row 3**. Press [ENTER] (Windows) [RETURN] (Macintosh). **Note:** A box will be drawn *around* the cells, they won't be shaded.

=AVERAGE(C3:L3)

4. **#DIV/0!** appears in the cell. To prove that it is not an error, **type two grades in cells to the right**. An average appears in cell B3.

5. Use **AutoFill** to put this average into as many cells as you have students. Each cell will read **#DIV/0!**, but you know it's OK.

B	C		B	C
Average	1		Average	1
#DIV/0!			80	80

Formatting Cells

1. Click the **Column B Indicator** to select the column.

2001 only

2. In the **Formatting Palette**, click the **Format** menu and choose **Number**.

3. Click the **Decrease Decimals** button in the **Formatting Palette**, to choose **1** place after the decimal.

4. **Delete** the **grades** you entered to test the formula.

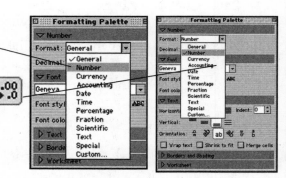

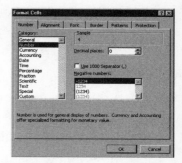

2000, 98, & 97

2. Click the **Format** menu and choose **Cells**. Choose **Number**, then **0** in **Decimal places.**

4. **Delete** the **grades** you entered to test the formula.

Inserting a Header

1. Click the **View** menu and choose **Header and Footer.**

2. Click the **Custom Header** button.

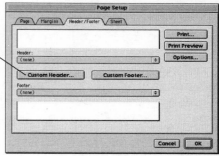

3. Type a "**Reading Grades**" in the center box.

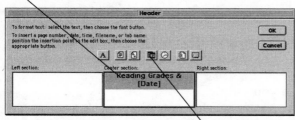

4. Press the **Spacebar**, then click the **Insert Date** button.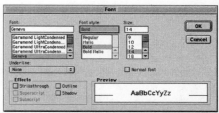

5. **Select the text** and click the **Font** button. **A**

6. Choose **Bold** from **Font style** and **14** from **Size**. Click **OK.**

7. Click **OK**, then click the **Page** tab.

8. Choose **Landscape** then click **OK**. Click **OK** to return to the gradebook. **Note:** The header won't show until you print the file.

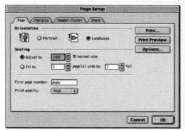

Filling Cells with Color

Sometimes it's difficult to read data across a wide worksheet. Adding color to every other row can make this easier.

1. Click the **Row 3 Header** to select the entire row.

2. Press **CTRL** (Windows) **⌘** (Macintosh) and click the **Row 5 Indicator**. Using this method, select every other row.

2001 only

3. Click the arrow next to **Borders and Shading** on the **Formatting Palette**. Click the **Fill color** box and choose a **light pastel color**. Skip to Step 4.

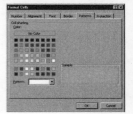

2000, 98, & 97

3. Click the **Format** menu and choose **Cells**. Click the **Patterns** tab and choose a light pastel color, then click **OK.**

4. **Click to deselect** the rows. The rows are filled with color.

Freezing Panes

Eventually you will have so many grades that you'll need to scroll to the right side to see them all. When this happens, you won't be able to see the student names or averages. Splitting the worksheet window allows you to see both parts at the same time.

1. Click the **Column C Indicator** to select the column.

2. Click the **Window** menu and choose **Freeze Panes**. A vertical line appears.

3. **Click the right scroll arrow** to see how a pane works. As you scroll right, the columns slide under the pane, under the Student and Average columns. This lets you see whose grades you are looking at when you are on

	A	B	E	F	G	H
1	Student	Average	3	4	5	6
2						
3		#DIV/0!				
4		#DIV/0!				
5		#DIV/0!				
6		#DIV/0!				

page 2. **Note:** To unfreeze a pane, click the **Windows** menu and choose **Unfreeze Panes.**

Protecting Cells

1. You need to lock the cells containing formulas so you won't accidentally type in them. We'll protect (lock) the entire worksheet, but first you need to *unlock* the cells where you need to type. Click the **Column A Indicator**. Press [CTRL] (Windows) [⌘] (Macintosh) and click the **Column C Indicator** and **drag right** to select columns in which you will type grades. Pressing [CTRL] (Windows) [⌘] (Macintosh) allows you to select noncontiguous cells.

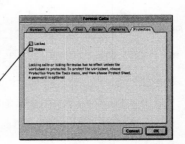

2. Click the **Format** menu, choose **Cells**, then the **Protection** tab. Click **Locked** to remove the checkmark from the box. Click **OK**.

3. Click the **Tools** menu, choose **Protection**, then **Worksheet**. Click **OK**. You can password-protect the worksheet, but you don't have to. Remember, you'll have to enter the password *every* time you open the file.

If you enter a password, be sure it's a password you'll remember. If you forget it, you won't be able to open the file! It's also case sensitive, so remember if you use any capital letters!

Removing the Column and Row Headers

Worksheets don't always look like worksheets. Changing the display options and adding color can make them look more professional.

1. Click the **Edit** menu and choose **Preferences**. Versions 2000 and 97 click the **Tools** menu and choose **Options**. Version 98, click the **Tools** menu and choose **Preferences**.

2. Click to remove the checkmarks from **Row & Column Headers**. Click **OK**.

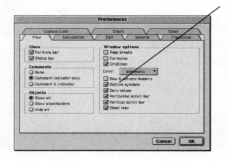
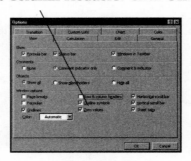

3. Click a cell with a formula, type a number, then press **ENTER** (Windows) **RETURN** (Macintosh). A message reminding you that the cell is protected appears.

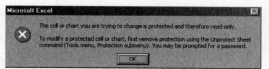

Password-Protecting the File

1. Click the **File** menu and choose **Save As**.

2. Click the **Options** button. In Version 2000 click the **Tools** menu and choose **General Options**.

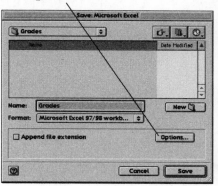

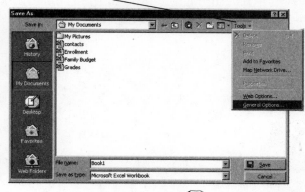

3. Type a password in the **Password to open** box. Click **OK** or press **ENTER** (Windows) **RETURN** (Macintosh).

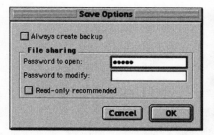

4. Reenter the password and click **OK** or press **ENTER** (Windows) **RETURN** (Macintosh).

5. **Close** the file.

Opening a Password-Protected File

1. **Open** the file.

2. **Type the password** *exactly* as you did when you set it.

3. Click **OK** or press **ENTER** (Windows) **RETURN** (Macintosh).

You'll see this message if you password-protected the file.

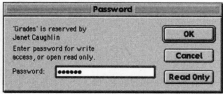

You'll also see this message if you chose Password to modify.

*If you enter a password in **Password to modify**, the file opens as read only unless you enter the password.*

*If you click **Read-only Recommended**, when you open the file you must choose whether to open the file as read-only or with the ability to save changes.*

*Click **Always create backup** to ensure that you have another copy if your computer crashes while the file is open.*

*Be **sure** it's a password you'll remember. If you forget it, you won't be able to open the file! It's also case sensitive, so remember if you use any capital letters!*

Creating a Student Address Database with *AppleWorks*

AppleWorks is an integrated suite of programs that includes a word processor, a drawing program, a painting program, a database program, and a spreadsheet program. The book *AppleWorkshop for Teachers* by Janet Caughlin includes step-by-step instructions for using *AppleWorks* to create slide show presentations; generate budgets, charts, and graphs; create worksheets and newsletters; build Web pages; and much more. The following walkthrough, reprinted from *AppleWorkshop for Teachers,* refers to the database tool within *AppleWorks.*

Create a New Database

Make an Address Database

A database will allow you to organize large amounts of information and make changes with a few keystrokes. An address book is a common example of a database. It contains fields of information like first name, last name, address, city, state, zip, and phone number. It also contains records, the data entered in each field for each person.

> ### This Activity Covers the Following Topics
> * Defining a Database
> * Entering Data
> * Saving the File
> * Duplicating a Record
> * Sorting Data
> * Finding Records
> * Making a New Layout
> * Editing a Layout
> * Viewing the Records in List View
> * Changing the Font Characteristics
> * Changing the Field Order

Defining a Database

1. Create a new Database file. The **Define Database Fields** dialog box appears. This lets you decide the fields or categories for your database. This database will have the fields "First Name," "Last Name," "Street," "City," "State," "Zip," and "Phone."

2. Type "**First Name**" in the **Field Name** box. The Create button becomes black (active) with a double line around it when you start typing. This is a text field, and text is chosen as the field type. Click the **Create** button (or press RETURN (Macintosh) ENTER (Windows) since Create has a double ring around it).

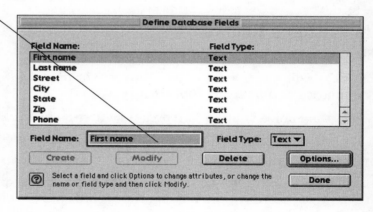

3. Type "**Last Name**" in the **Field Name** box — just type over the words First Name. Click Create or press RETURN (Macintosh) ENTER (Windows).

4. Create the fields **Street**, **City**, **State**, **Zip**, and **Phone**. All are text fields.

5. Click **Done**.

If you make a typing mistake, don't worry! Click the field name. Type the right name and click Modify.

If you find you forgot a field, click the Layout menu and choose Define Fields and type it in. This new field will go at the end of the list.

Entering Data

1. Click in the text box next to the **First Name**. Type "**Julie.**"

2. Press `TAB` to move to the next field, **Last Name**.

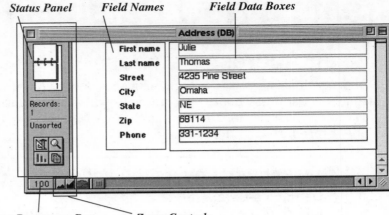

Status Panel — *Field Names* — *Field Data Boxes*

You could also click in the field, but it is faster to keep your hands on the keyboard.

Zoom Percentage Box
Tells size of Window being viewed. You can also change the size here.

Zoom Controls
Makes size of window smaller or larger.

3. Type "**Thomas**" and **press** `TAB`. Enter the remaining data in this record, pressing `TAB` between each field.

4. To create a new record, click the **New Record** button,  press `⌘R` (Macintosh) `CTRL R` (Windows), or click the **Edit** menu and choose **New Record.** Enter data for four people.

Press the Tab key if you don't see the Field Data Boxes.

Saving the File

1. Click the **File** menu and choose **Save**, or press `⌘S` (Macintosh) `CTRL S` (Windows).

2. Name the file "**Address.**" Always give a file a logical name that reflects what is in it.

Duplicating a Record

1. **Click** anywhere in the **Julie Thomas record**.

2. Click the **Edit** menu and choose **Duplicate** or press `⌘D` (Macintosh) `CTRL D` (Windows). A duplicate of the record appears as Record 5.

3. Select the name "**Julie**" and type a new first name. Now you have two Thomas records.

Sorting Data

Sorting means alphabetizing or putting the records in a different order. The Status Panel indicates there are five records in the file and the records are unsorted.

1. Click the **Organize** menu and choose **Sort Records** or press `⌘J` (Macintosh) `CTRL J` (Windows) to sort the data. The phrase, *Juggle the Order*, may help you remember the key command.

2. A dialog box appears. **Sort Order** is empty — waiting for you to decide which field you want to use for the sorting. Click the field **Last Name.** When it is selected, click the **Move** button. The field Last Name appears in the Sort Order box.

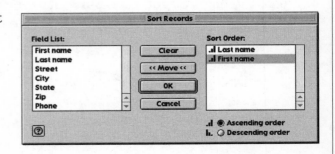

3. **Double-click First Name** to move this field to the Sort Order box. Double-clicking eliminates the need to click the Move button. This procedure will sort the records by Last Name and then by First Name. If two people have the same last name, they will be in order by the first name, e.g., the Thomas records. Click the **OK** button.

4. The Status Panel says **Sorted** below the Book icon. Use the Scroll Bar to see that the records are sorted.

Finding Records

1. Click the **Find** button or click the **Layout** menu and choose **Find**. You could also press [SHIFT][⌘][F] (Macintosh) [SHIFT][CTRL][F] (Windows).

2. A dialog box appears similar to the screen for entering data. The Status Panel looks different though. Look for the **Find** button. Type "**Julie**" in the **First Name** field data box. Press [TAB]. Type "**Thomas**" in the **Last Name** field.

3. Press [RETURN] (Macintosh) [ENTER] (Windows) or click the **Find** button. "**1 (5)**" appears under Records: to indicate that one record out of five met the Find criteria.

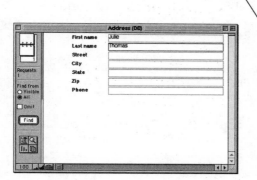
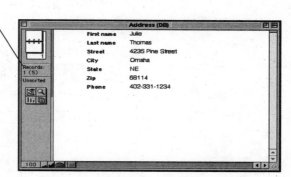

4. Click the **Organize** menu and choose **Show All Records** or press [SHIFT][⌘][A] (Macintosh) [SHIFT][CTRL][A] (Windows). All five records will reappear. The number "5" appears under **Records:** on the Status Panel to indicate you're looking at all records.

Making a New Layout

1. Click the **Layout Popup icon** on the gray **Status Panel** and choose **New Layout**. You could also click the **Layout** menu and choose **New Layout**.

2. Name the layout "**Phone List.**" Click the **Columnar report** button. Click the **OK** button or press [RETURN] (Macintosh) [ENTER] (Windows).

3. Hold down [SHIFT], and click the fields **First Name** and **Last Name**. Click **Move**. These field names will move into the **Field Order** box. Double-click the field **Phone** to add it to the Field Order box. Click **OK** or press [RETURN] (Macintosh) [ENTER] (Windows).

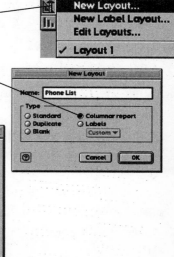
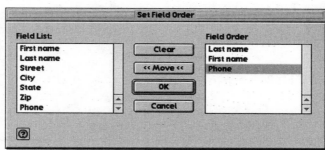

Your records appear in a column. Only the fields First Name, Last Name, and Phone appear because those were the only fields you inserted into the layout.

4. Click the **Layout** button or click the **Layout** menu and choose **Layout**.
   Layout allows you to make changes to the looks of the database layout you are using (Phone list in this case). Field Names and Field Data boxes for one record appear. The Layout mode looks like the Drawing portion of *AppleWorks* because you see a grid and drawing tools. You can move field data boxes and field titles to fit your needs, change fonts, font sizes, styles of print, and add graphics. **Click the gray Body box** and **move the Body line down slightly**.

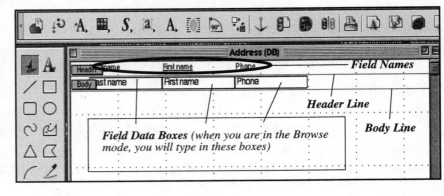

5. Click the **Layout** menu and choose **Browse**. You can also press [SHIFT] [⌘] [B] (Macintosh) [SHIFT] [CTRL] [B] (Windows).

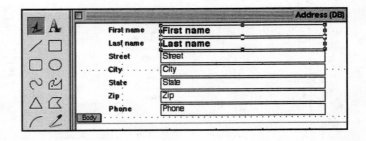

Anything above the Header line will appear on the top of each page. Everything above the Body line will be data. The same amount of space between the Field Data Boxes and the Body Line will appear between each record in the database.

You make changes to the Look of the database in the Layout mode. Remember the "L" means change the looks. You enter or edit data in the Browse mode.

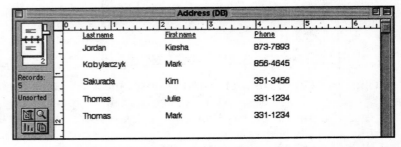

All records appear. The Field Titles are at the top of the page, the data is below the titles, and the space between each record is equal to the space you inserted when you moved the Body Line.

Editing a Layout

1. Click the **Layout** icon and choose **Layout 1**.

2. Click the **Layout** button or choose **Layout**. You can also press [SHIFT] [⌘] [L] (Macintosh) [SHIFT] [CTRL] [L] (Windows).

3. Click the **First Name data box**. Press [SHIFT] and click **Last Name data box**. Both have handles.

4. Click the **Layout** menu and choose **Size**, then **14 Point**.

5. Click the **Layout** menu and choose **Style**, then **Bold**.

6. Click the **Layout** menu and choose **Browse**, or [SHIFT] [⌘] [B] (Macintosh) [SHIFT] [CTRL] [B] (Windows) to see how easy it is to distinguish between records.

7. Click the **Save** button, or click the **File** menu and choose **Save**, or press [⌘] [S] (Macintosh) [CTRL] [S] (Windows).

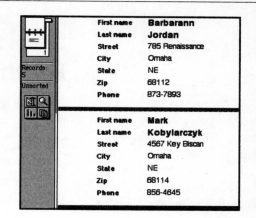

Viewing the Records in List View

1. Click the **List** button  or click the **Layout** menu and choose **List**. All records and fields are shown in this mode.

2. The data in the **Street** column may be cut off. It's really easy to fix. Place the cursor on the line between the field names **Street** and **City**.

```
Street        ⟷ City
```

3. When the cursor turns into a **crosshair**, press the mouse button and drag to the right to increase the column width for the **Street** field.

4. Using this procedure, make the **State** and **Zip** fields more narrow.

Changing the Font Characteristics

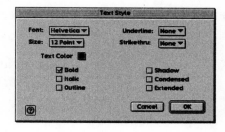

1. **Double-click** the field name for **First Name**.

2. **Click the box** next to the word **Bold**. Click **OK** to see the changes.

Changing the Field Order

1. Place the cursor in the **middle** of the field name for **Phone**.

2. When the cursor turns into a **crosshair with a box in the center**, press the mouse button and **drag to the left until the cursor is on top of the Street field**. Release the mouse button. The **Phone** field is in front of the **Street** field.

```
Phone ◀▣▶
```

First name	Last name	Street	City	State	Zip	Phone
Kiesha	Jordan	785 Renaissance	Omaha	NE	68112	873-7893
Mark	Kobylarczyk	4567 Key Biscan	Omaha	NE	68114	856-4645
Kim	Sakurada	12245 127 Ave	Omaha	NE	68115	351-3456
Julie	Thomas	4235 Pine Street	Omaha	NE	68114	331-1234
Mark	Thomas	4235 Pine Street	Omaha	NE	68114	331-1234

Before

First name	Last name	Phone	Street	City	State	Zip
Kiesha	Jordan	873-7893	785 Renaissance	Omaha	NE	68112
Mark	Kobylarczyk	856-4645	4567 Key Biscan	Omaha	NE	68114
Kim	Sakurada	351-3456	12245 127 Ave	Omaha	NE	68115
Julie	Thomas	331-1234	4235 Pine Street	Omaha	NE	68114
Mark	Thomas	331-1234	4235 Pine Street	Omaha	NE	68114

After

You can make your own worksheets and puzzles today! Log on to the Tom Snyder Productions Web site and sign up for a free trial of the Essentials programs.

www.tomsnyder.com/weaving

Sample Worksheets and Puzzles from *Essential Tools for Teachers*

Essential Tools for Teachers is a series of timesaving tools that you can use to easily create worksheets, puzzles, tests, quizzes, and flashcards. The programs are available both on CD-ROM and as an Internet subscription. On the following pages, you'll find examples of worksheets created with the *Essential Tools for Teachers* programs that you can reproduce and use in your classroom. Answer keys are below.

Presidents of the United States Word Search Answer Key

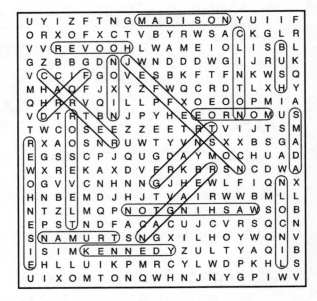

Rounding Numbers Practice Worksheet Answer Key

Round each number to the nearest ten.

1. 18 **20**
2. 818 **820**
3. 223 **220**
4. 695 **700**
5. 371 **370**

Round each number to the nearest hundred.

6. 528 **500**
7. 8,508 **8,500**
8. 8,397 **8,400**
9. 2,105 **2,100**
10. 4,854 **4,900**

Round each number to the nearest thousand.

11. 18 **0**
12. 18,488 **18,000**
13. 85,907 **86,000**
14. 84,084 **84,000**
15. 46,366 **46,000**

Round each number to the nearest ten thousand.

16. 514,726 **510,000**
17. 778,551 **780,000**
18. 868,092 **870,000**
19. 679,966 **680,000**
20. 692,993 **690,000**

Presidents of the United States Word Search

This word search was made with *Essential Word Puzzles*. The program allows you to choose a puzzle size and select whether to include reverse words and diagonal words. In addition to word searches, with *Essential Word Puzzles* you can easily make crosswords, cryptograms, 'kriss-kross' puzzles, and quote falls.

Name_____ Date_____

United States Presidents

Use the word list below to find hidden words in the puzzle. When you find a word in the puzzle, draw a circle around it. Words can be displayed in a straight line forwards, backwards, up, down, or diagonally.

```
U Y I Z F T N G M A D I S O N Y U I I F
O R X O F X C T V B Y R W S A C K G L R
V V R E V O O H L W A M E I O L I S B L
G Z B B G D N J W N D D D W G I J R U K
V C C I F G O V E S B K F T F N K W S Q
M H A O F J X Y Z F W Q C R D T L X H Y
Q H R R V Q I L L P F X O E O O P M I A
V D T R T B N J P Y H E E O R N O M U S
T W C O S E E Z Z E E T R T V I J T S M
R X A O S N R U W T Y V N S X X B S G A
E G S S C P J Q U G D A Y M O C H U A D
W X R E K A X D V F R K B R S N C D W A
O G V V C N H N N G J H E W L F I Q N X
H N B E M D J H J T V A I R W W B M L L
N T Z L M Q P N O T G N I H S A W S O B
E P S T N D F A C A C U J C V R S Q C N
S N A M U R T S N G X I L H O Y W Q N V
I S I M K E N N E D Y Z U L T Y A Q I B
E H L L U I K P M R C Y L W D P K H L S
U I X O M T O N Q W H N J N Y G P I W V
```

WASHINGTON	GRANT	NIXON
ADAMS	HOOVER	FORD
JEFFERSON	ROOSEVELT	CARTER
MADISON	TRUMAN	REAGAN
MONROE	EISENHOWER	BUSH
LINCOLN	KENNEDY	CLINTON

Rounding Numbers Practice Worksheet

This worksheet was made with *Essential Math Worksheets*. The program automatically generates worksheets on basic computation, shapes, money, time, fractions, rounding, and place values. You can easily customize the worksheets to make them appropriate for your students.

Name _____   **Date** _____

Round each number to the nearest ten.

1. 18 _____   2. 818 _____

3. 223 _____   4. 695 _____

5. 371 _____

Round each number to the nearest hundred.

6. 528 _____   7. 8,508 _____

8. 8,397 _____   9. 2,105 _____

10. 4,854 _____

Round each number to the nearest thousand.

11. 18 _____   12. 18,488 _____

13. 85,907 _____   14. 84,084 _____

15. 46,366 _____

Round each number to the nearest ten thousand.

16. 514,726 _____   17. 778,551 _____

18. 868,092 _____   19. 679,966 _____

20. 692,993 _____

Creating a School Year Time Line with *TimeLiner*

Visit the Tom Snyder Productions Web site to download a demo version of TimeLiner *to use with this walkthrough.*
www.tomsnyder.com/weaving

TimeLiner is a software program that makes it easy to create, illustrate, and print time lines. The program automatically organizes events into chronological order and allows you to print your time line in list or banner format. You can also use *TimeLiner*'s slide show feature and graphics library to create and present a multimedia slide show of your time line.

Below are instructions for creating a basic time line with *TimeLiner*, and also a reproducible sample time line printed from the program.

Goal

To create a time line of the school year calendar.

Get Started

1. To get the demo software, go to **http://www.tomsnyder.com/weaving** and click *TimeLiner* Demo.

2. Follow the online instructions to download the free demo version of *TimeLiner* 5.0 for your platform (Macintosh or Windows).

3. Once you have completed the download, double-click the *TimeLiner* 5.0 Demo folder on your computer and then double-click the *TimeLiner* 5.0 Demo icon.

Note: If you do not have *QuickTime* installed on your computer, you will need to install it to view videos on *TimeLiner* 5.0.

4. Click Start and then click New to begin.

Create a New Time Line

1. Click to select Yearly/Monthly and then click OK.

2. From the Format menu, choose Date Format. Under Start the Year, choose August, and then click OK.

3. Type "August 28" in the box directly under When. Press the Tab key and type "First day of school" in the box directly under What.

4. Press the Return/Enter key. Type "June 22." Press the Tab key and type "Last day of school."

5. Press the Return/Enter key twice and type "November 22." Press the Tab key and type "Thanksgiving Break." Notice this event has been placed in chronological order, above June 22.

6. Press the Return/Enter key twice and type "February 19." Press the Tab key and type "Presidents' Day."

7. Continue to add other dates and events until you have six to eight entries.

Edit and Delete Events

1. Click on the November 22 event to select it.

2. Now click Edit on the clock menu (on the left side of your screen). The Edit Event box opens, enabling you to edit your event.

3. Click the box next to the word "to" and enter an end date of November 28.

4. Click OK; notice an End column has appeared.

5. Click another event and click Delete on the clock. Click Cancel, since you really don't want to delete this event. If you mistakenly delete an event, you can choose Undo Delete from the Edit menu (only right after you delete it). Deleting removes an event permanently from all five views of a time line.

The Five Views

You can view the information you've entered in five ways: Data, Banner, Compact, List, and Slideshow. To switch between views, simply click the little icons near the top left of the screen. When you enter data, it is entered automatically into all five views. Try each view now.

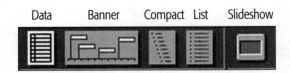

Expand and Compress Your Time Line

While in Banner view, click Expand on the clock a few times; watch your time line grow. Now click Compress and watch it shrink.

Enhance Your Time Line

1. While in Banner view, click the "First day of school" banner to select it.

2. Click the Choose Font button **A** at the top of the screen. The Choose Font box opens. Choose a font, font style, size, and color for this event. Click OK. Notice the changes on that banner.

3. Banners can be moved vertically by clicking and dragging them to the desired location.

4. With the First Day of School banner still selected, click the Edit Flag Style button [icon] at the top of the screen. The Edit Flag Style dialog box opens, allowing you to customize the shape and color of the flag.

5. To add dates to the Banner view, select Add Date to Text from the Format menu. Notice the event dates now appear in the banners.

Add Labels

1. While in Banner view, click Label on the clock to add a title to the time line.

2. Type "School Calendar" and click OK. Move the title by clicking and dragging the text box.

3. Change the font by clicking the Choose Font button while the title is highlighted.

Add Graphics

1. Click Graphic on the clock. Click OK. The Add Graphic dialog box opens.

2. Double-click the graphic of Abraham Lincoln.

3. You can move the graphic by clicking and dragging it. You can also resize the graphic by dragging one of its corners inward or outward.

Add Multimedia, Notes, and Web Links to Your Time Line

1. Click to select the "Presidents' Day" banner and then click Edit on the clock.

2. In the Edit Event box, click the Picture or Movie tab and then click Import.

3. Click Presidents 1 and then click George Washington. Click OK.

4. Click the Notes tab. In the Notes box, type "The First American President."

5. Click the Web Link tab and type "www.whitehouse.gov/history/presidents/gw1.html" and then click OK.

6. Add notes, multimedia, and Web links to some of your other banners by following the above steps 1–5.

View Your Time Line as a Slide Show

1. Click the Slideshow view icon at the top of the screen.

2. Banners with multimedia elements attached will be much more interesting to view as slides, so you may decide to click Only Show Events with Media Attachments.

3. Choose a Background color and then click Run Slideshow.

4. To advance to the next slide, click Next in the lower right corner.

5. To view Web links, click the Web Link button and your browser will open to the Web page if you have a live Internet connection.

6. Press the ESC key on your keyboard to exit the slide show.

Extensions

1. View pre-made time lines. Choose Open from the File menu, navigate to the *TimeLiner* 5.0 Demo folder, and then click Sample Me Time Line or the folder entitled Sample Time Lines.

2. Want some great classroom ideas using *TimeLiner?* Check out *TimeLiner* Online at: **www.tomsnyder.com/classroom/timelineronline/index.asp.**

Sample Time Line: Celsius and Fahrenheit

You can use *TimeLiner* to represent a lot more than historical events. Below is a sample time line representing the relationship between Celsius and Fahrenheit temperatures that you can reproduce and use in your classroom.

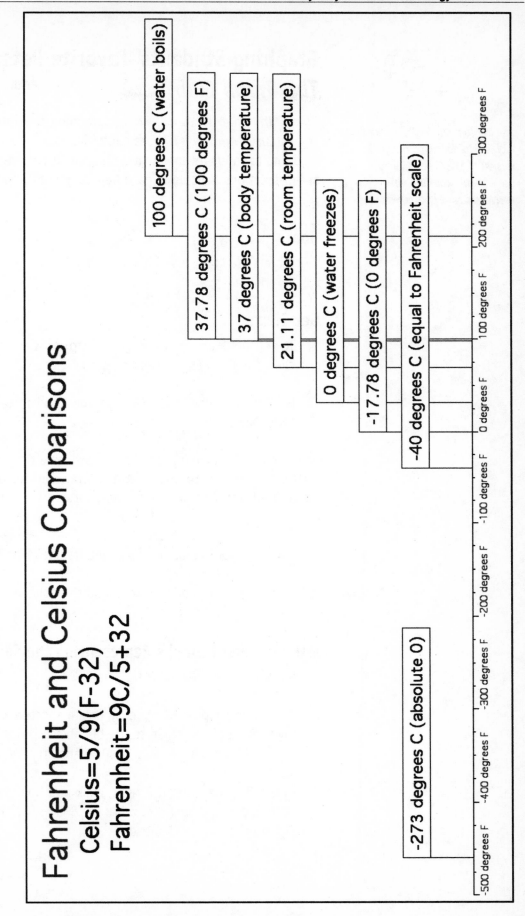

Fahrenheit and Celsius Comparisons

Celsius=5/9(F-32)
Fahrenheit=9C/5+32

100 degrees C (water boils)

37.78 degrees C (100 degrees F)

37 degrees C (body temperature)

21.11 degrees C (room temperature)

0 degrees C (water freezes)

-17.78 degrees C (0 degrees F)

-40 degrees C (equal to Fahrenheit scale)

-273 degrees C (absolute 0)

-500 degrees F -400 degrees F -300 degrees F -200 degrees F -100 degrees F 0 degrees F 100 degrees F 200 degrees F 300 degrees F

Visit the Tom Snyder Productions Web site to download a demo version of The Graph Club *to use with this walkthrough.*
www.tomsnyder.com/weaving

Graphing Students' Favorite Pets with *The Graph Club*

The Graph Club is an easy-to-use graphing program designed for grades K–4. You can use *The Graph Club* to construct colorful, child-friendly graphs and teach students to interpret information displayed on different types of graphs. Below are instructions for creating a simple graph with *The Graph Club*.

Goal

To create a graph representing students' pets.

Get Started

1. To get the demo software, go to **http://www.tomsnyder.com/weaving** and click *The Graph Club* Demo.

2. Follow the online instructions to download a free demo version of *The Graph Club* Demo for the Macintosh.

Note: The Graph Club full version is available for both Macintosh and Windows platforms. Go to **http://www.tomsnyder.com** for more information and to get a free 45-day trial version of the software.

3. Once you have completed the download, double-click *The Graph Club* Demo folder on your computer and then double-click *The Graph Club* Demo icon.

4. Click anywhere on the screen and then click Skip Introduction.

Make Different Graphs Representing the Same Information

1. Click Explore, then click OK.

2. Two empty graphs will open. To create a Picture Graph on the left graph, drag the symbol of the cat from the bin above into the cat column below. Notice the Bar Graph on the right. Both graphs represent the same data.

3. In the Bar Graph on the right, click and hold the top line of the bar representing cats and drag upward to the 8 line. Notice that the information in the Picture Graph also changed.

4. Repeat the above steps to create a graph that represents the following: 8 cats, 5 rabbits, 2 turtles, and 9 dogs.

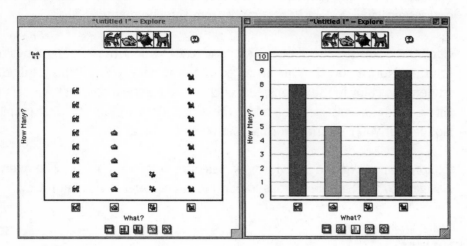

5. This data can be displayed in five ways, each represented by a symbol at the bottom of the graph: ▦ ▦ ▐▌▐ ▨ ▧ Table, Picture, Bar, Line, and Circle. Click each button to see the different graphs.

6. While in the Circle Graph, click the number that represents the dogs. The How should we label our circle? box appears. Click the circle next to 50%, and then click OK. Notice that the Circle Graph is now labeled in percentages.

Create a New Graph

1. Select Close Set from the File menu. Click Create, then click OK. Select Choose Symbols from the Graph menu.

2. Scroll through the list of pictures and choose four new symbols. To select a new symbol, click and hold on the picture and drag it up to the bin at the top of the screen to replace the old symbol. Once you've replaced all 4 symbols, click OK.

3. Click the first zero in the How Many? box on the graph. Type in the number, then click OK. Repeat this step for all 4 symbols. To see the data in different graph types, choose Make Another Graph from the Graph menu. Use the buttons at the bottom of the graph to see the data in the different formats.

Additional Tips and Information

1. Although printing is disabled in the Demo, you can view the different print options available. Select Print Graphs from the File menu.

2. Click the boxes next to Table, Bar, and Circle to select these graph types for printing. Notice how they are arranged on the preview page. If you want your students to color in the graphs, just click in the box next to Don't Fill Bars or Circle Wedges. You can also add a Title and Description for your graphs. Notice that you can print Normal, Big Book, or Poster size.

3. Explore sample graph activities by selecting Open from the File menu. Navigate to the Sample Graphs folder and choose an activity to preview.

Extensions

What are ways that you could integrate *The Graph Club* into your classroom curriculum? List your ideas below.

_____

_____

_____

_____

_____

Creating Cooperative Groups

Creating good cooperative groups can be one of the most difficult and most important parts of any cooperative learning activity. When I first started teaching, I let students pick their own teams. It was easier on me, and besides, I wanted students to like me. I quickly learned, however, that a few children were always left groupless. Plus, the groups of friends who gathered often wanted to talk about everything but the discussion topic I'd assigned. In reality, once students enter the workforce, they won't have the opportunity to pick their coworkers. They need to learn to get along with those they might not know and even might not like. As I discovered, it's important to be thoughtful about putting together student groups.

Here's one method that might make the process a little easier. Make a chart and write each of your students' names in one of four columns — Strong, Above Average, Average, or Weak — depending on his or her academic ability. This is, of course, a very subjective process, but do the best you can. Then attempt to make each column of names the same length by moving students to the left or right according to their social maturity. By thus juggling students, you will eventually have columns of roughly equal length. A team of four students can then be built by choosing one name from each column.

Strong	Above Average	Average	Weak
Jill	Bob	Jeff	Sam
Tina	Beth	Arthur	
		Andy →	

After you've made the initial division of your class into groups, review the teams and make sure they are balanced by ethnicity, race, and gender. (Teams will rarely be balanced on the first try.) Finally, look for irreconcilable trouble spots, where two students simply can't be sitting next to one another. Remember, though, that cooperative experiences can provide excellent mechanisms to get formerly combative students working together. Rather than rearranging groups immediately, you may want to simply highlight the potential trouble areas and be prepared to provide extra support through the group experiences.

Once you have formed groups, I also recommend reminding students about the rules for working together. Although cooperative learning has grown in popularity over the last couple of decades, group work remains a new approach for many students and teachers. Children who have experienced only whole class and individualized instruction can be lost when thrown into a group of peers. Students need to be told how to work in groups, and need many opportunities to practice in different contexts. Whether you post them on the wall or give students a handout, the rules for teamwork and polite behavior when working in groups — don't interrupt, be a good listener, no put-downs, and so on — should be explicit and clear to all students.

Large-Scale Display Systems

When using the computer as a tool for whole-class instruction, it's helpful to have a large-scale display system in place. This helps focus students' attention and ensures that everyone can see the information you're presenting. The four main display options — scan converters, TV/computer monitor combinations, LCD palettes, and projection systems — vary in size, price, and ease of use.

Scan Converter

Probably the least expensive and most portable option for enlarging your computer display is an external scan converter. This device, which typically costs between $100 and $250*, connects your computer to a large TV monitor and translates the video signal from the computer into a type of signal acceptable to a television. You'll need to supply the monitor yourself, but you're bound to find one attached to a VCR if nowhere else.

Usually an external scan converter is a small box with plugs for "video in" and "video out." One cable runs from the computer to the scan converter box. Another cable runs from the box to the television. Once you know how to hook up the cables, it's easy to move the scan converter from computer to computer. Internal scan converters are also available: You can buy both TV monitors and computers that come with a scan converter installed.

The quality of the display will vary with the quality of the scan converter as well as the quality of the monitor. If possible, test various models with your particular setup before purchasing any for your school. Check especially how text looks on the TV monitor; that's usually where you'll see problems.

TV/Computer Monitor Combination

Another option is to purchase a computer with a large TV monitor instead of a computer monitor. You skip the process of hooking your computer to a TV monitor, because your television is your computer monitor! The monitor functions as a normal TV: You can watch cable as well as connect a VCR or a videodisc player. Once again, check quality before making any purchases.

LCD Palette

An LCD palette (LCD stands for liquid crystal display) is a device that uses an overhead projector to help display what's on the computer monitor. With an LCD palette, one cable extends between the video connector on your computer and the LCD palette. A second cable connects the palette to the computer monitor.

The palette sits on top of an overhead projector. Whatever appears on the computer monitor also appears on the palette, and the overhead projects that image onto a big screen (or a white wall). It can be a nice setup, but the image quality varies greatly with the quality of the LCD palette and the overhead projector. In addition, you often have to turn down the lights to get a clear picture, and a darkened room full of students can have its own negative consequences. Alternatively, you could buy an LCD projector. This device is simply a combination of an LCD palette and an overhead projector. The advantage is that the bulb in this kind of projector is better — it sounds simple, but you'll notice a difference in brightness and image quality. LCD palettes cost $2000–$4000, and LCD projectors cost $2000–$8000.* Keep checking for the latest information on these products, as technology is always changing.

Projection System

Top-of-the-line projection systems, which accept video and audio output from your computer and project both of them, are available but costly. While prices for these systems have been dropping, you can still spend $3000–$5000* for a good one. Projection systems are particularly suited to very large groups, so they might be overkill for your classroom.

No matter which option you choose, look before you buy. Then weigh the costs against the expected benefits. What's right for one classroom may not be the best solution for yours.

* approximate prices as of January 2002

Creating a Classroom Rules Slide Show with *PowerPoint*

Using Microsoft PowerPoint, you can create your own multimedia slide shows. The following walk through is reprinted from the book PowerPoint Workshop for Teachers by Janet Caughlin. In addition to step-by-step instructions for creating slide shows and handouts with PowerPoint, the book includes tips and advice from classroom teachers, as well as a CD-ROM packed with clip art, templates, and sample files.

Create a Basic Slide Presentation with a Summary Slide

A Classroom Rules Slide Show

Kids will pay attention if you use a *PowerPoint* slide show to emphasize important points. It's a fun way to convey information and to get students' attention. Another benefit of using *PowerPoint* is that your presentations are so easy to edit.

This Activity Covers the Following Topics:

- Creating a Presentation Using a Design Template
- Creating a Title Slide
- Inserting a New Slide
- Creating a Text & Clip Art Slide
- Inserting a New Slide
- Formatting Text
- Inserting New Slides
- Checking the Spelling
- Creating a Summary Slide (Windows only)
- Changing the Order of Slides
- Creating a Summary Slide (Macintosh only)
- Saving the Slide Show Presentation
- Using Custom Animation
  -  XP only
  - X and 2001 only
  - 2000 only
  - 97 and 98 only

Creating a Presentation Using a Design Template

The screen you see when you launch *PowerPoint* depends on the version you are using. **Find your version and follow the directions.**

 XP only

Click the **Design button**, then **click a design**.

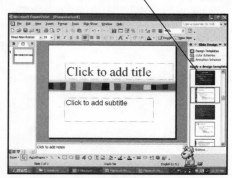

 **X and 2001 only**

Click the **arrow** to the left of **Presentations** in the **Project Gallery**.

Click **Designs** and then **double-click** a **design** from the gallery to the right.

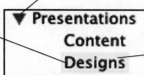

▼ Presentations
Content
Designs

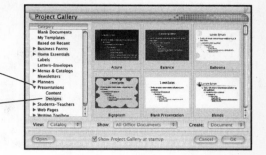

2000, 97 and ☀ 98 only

Click **Template**. Click the **Design Templates tab**, then **double-click** a **design**.

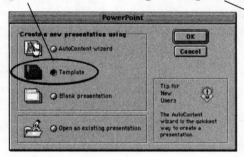

Creating a Title Slide

1. XP versions may skip this step and move to the next step. The **Title Slide** layout is selected. Press `ENTER` (Windows) `RETURN` (Macintosh), or click **OK**. A slide formatted with a text box for a title and another text box for subtitles appears.

2. **Type** the words **Know the Rules.** The words appear in the top box reading **Click to add title.**

3. Click the bottom box reading **Click to add subtitle.** Type the words **A Quick Review.**

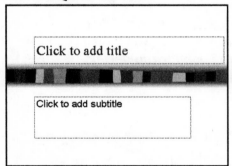

Inserting a New Slide

1. Click the **New Slide** icon

   or

   Choose **New Slide** from the **Insert** menu

   or

   Press `CTRL``M` (Windows) `⌘``M` (Macintosh).

XP, 2000, 97
☀ 98   ☀ X, 2001

Now you will make a slide for each rule. Each slide will have a rule and a picture.

2. Double-click the **Title, Text, and Content** or **Text & Clip Art** slide. The title varies according to the version of *PowerPoint* that you are using. This slide is formatted so you can write text on the left side and insert clip art on the right side.

2000, 97
98

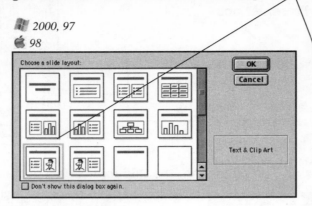

Creating a Text & Clip Art Slide

1. **Type** the words **Raise Your Hand.**

2. Click the bottom box, **Click to add text.** Type **When you have something to add to the class**.

3. Press **ENTER** (Windows) **RETURN** (Macintosh) and type **If you have a question**.

4. XP users click the **Clip Art icon** on the **right side of the slide. Other versions double-click the picture** to the right of the words.

If you decide you don't like the design you chose, click the Design button and you can choose a new one.

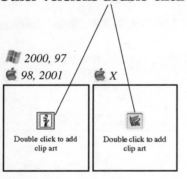

2000, 97
98, 2001   *X*

Double click to add clip art   Double click to add clip art

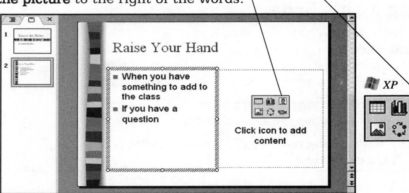

XP

In XP, the search box appears. *The Screen Beans shown in this activity work well with this presentation, but you can use other clip art pictures if you wish. Look for the perfect picture!*

5. Type **beans** in the box next to **Search text**, **Search for clips**, **Search**, or **Find** depending on the version of *PowerPoint* you are using. Double-click an image, or select the image and click the Insert or OK button. Use any picture you like.

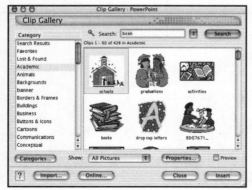

The clip art appears formatted to fit into the box.

Inserting a New Slide

XP, 2000, 97   98   X, 2001

1. Click the **New Slide** icon

   or

   Choose **New Slide** from the **Insert** menu

   or

   Press **CTRL M** (Windows) **⌘ M** (Macintosh).

2. **Double-click** the **Title, Content, and Text** or **Text & Clip Art** slide. The title varies according to the version of *PowerPoint* that you are using. This slide is the opposite of the one you just created. You can write text on the left side of the slide and insert clip art on the right side. Reversing the slide layout adds variety to a presentation.

Formatting Text

1. **Create** the slide below.

2. **Double-click** the word **"first"** to select it so you can emphasize this very important word.

3. Choose **Font** from the **Format** menu.

4. Click **the triangle** next to **Color** and choose more colors, then a **red** color.

5. Scroll under the **Size** menu and choose **36**.

6. Choose **Bold** in the **Font Style** box. Click **OK**.

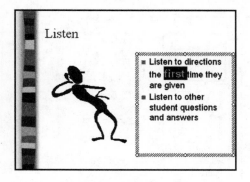

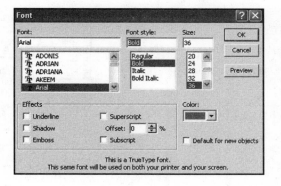

Inserting New Slides

Create the slides below using the steps above. Notice that some are Text & Clip Art slides and others are Clip Art & Text slides. You may choose the format yourself.

Checking the Spelling

1. Click the **Spelling** icon, press F7, or choose **Spelling** from the **Tools** menu.

   - If the program finds an incorrect spelling, select the correct spelling and then click **Change.**
   - If the program finds a correctly spelled word it doesn't recognize, click **Ignore**.
   - If the program finds a correctly spelled word it doesn't recognize and you use it frequently, click **Add** to add it to the dictionary.

2. Click **Close** or **OK** when you're finished.

Creating a Summary Slide (Windows only)

1. Click the **Slide Sorter** icon in the lower left corner or click the **View** menu and choose **Slide Sorter**. All of the slides appear in a small view.

2. **Click Slide 2, press [SHIFT], and click each slide** to select them.

3. Click the **Summary Slide icon** on the toolbar. You have just created a new slide that contains the titles of slides 2-6.

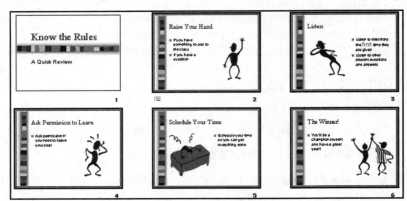

Changing the Order of Slides

1. Drag the **Summary Slide down** to the end.

2. Change the title from Summary Slide to **Follow These Rules**. You can add a graphic if you wish.

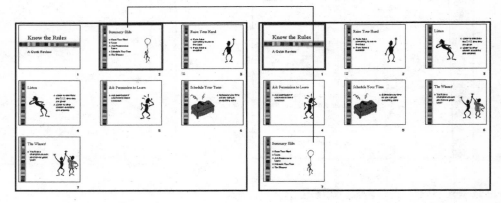

Creating a Summary Slide (Macintosh only)

1. Click the **Slide Sorter** icon in the lower left corner or click the **View** menu and choose **Slide Sorter**. All of the slides appear in a small view.

2. **Click Slide 6** in the Slide Sorter view. Create a **Text & Clip Art** slide.

3. **Double-click Slide 7**. Type **"Follow These Rules."**

4. Click the bulleted list section. Type the **title of each slide** as a **separate bullet**. Add **clip art on the right side**. Click the **Slide Sorter** icon in the lower left corner or click the **View** menu and choose **Slide Sorter**. All of the slides appear in a small view.

Saving the Slide Show Presentation

1. You've just made an awesome presentation! Save it on the hard drive or on a floppy disk.

2. **Run the slide show** to see how great it is.

Using Custom Animation

Now you're going to learn how to make a truly awesome slide show. Custom Animation is a more powerful way to animate text and pictures in your presentation. This lets you determine the order of appearance and sets the animation method for each element separately. Find your version of *PowerPoint* below and follow the appropriate instructions.

 XP only

This section is for PowerPoint XP users only. Users of other versions go to your section of this activity.

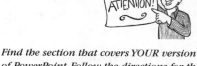

Adding Animations

1. **Double-click Slide 2** so it appears in full size.

2. **Click the graphic** to select it.

3. Click the **Slide Show menu** and choose **Custom Animation.**

4. Click the **Add Effects button** on the **Task Pane** and choose **Entrance**, then **Fly In**. This means that the graphic will fly in when the slide opens.

5. Choose **After Previous** in the **Start** choice. This means the graphic will appear automatically with the animation when the slide opens.

6. Choose **From Right** from the **Direction** choice. This means the graphic flies in from the right.

7. Click the **Play** button to see how the slide looks.

Find the section that covers YOUR version of PowerPoint. Follow the directions for that section. You are finished when you save the file.

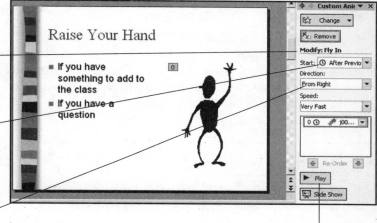

Adding Sound and Direction

1. Click the **text box** on the left side of the screen to select the entire box.

2. Click the **Add Effect button** on the **Task Pane** and choose **Entrance**, then **Fly In**. This means that the text will fly in when the slide opens.

3. You're going to leave **On Click** in the **Start** choice because you'll want to decide when the words appear on the screen by clicking the mouse. Notice that numbers have appeared telling you the order the elements were animated.

4. Click the **arrow** by the **second event** in the Animation task pane list. This is called the Animation Tag.

5. Choose **Effect Options**. A new window opens.

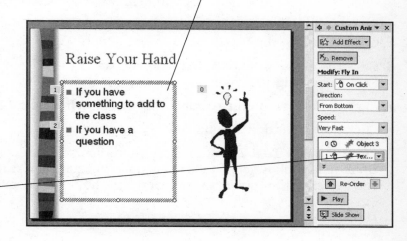

6. This window gives you animation choices you saw while animating the graphic, as well as some new ones. Choose **From Left** in the **Directions** choices.

7. Click the **arrow** by the **sound** box and make a choice. Click **OK**. You'll hear the sound.

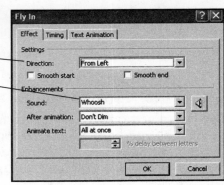

8. Click the **Slide Show button** on the **Task Pane** to see the slide show. Unlike the Play button, you must click the mouse to begin the animations where On Click was chosen. This is how the slide show will operate. Press the **Esc** key to stop the show.

9. Click the **Re-Order Up Arrow** on the Task Pane. This makes the clip art appear after the text. Click **Slide Show** to see the change. Click the **Animation Tag for the text**, then the **Down Arrow** to restore the order.

Animating the Remaining Slides

1. Scroll to **Slide 3**. Click the graphic.

2. Click the **Add Effects button** on the **Task Pane** and choose **Entrance**, then **Fly In**.

3. **Experiment with the buttons** to see what they do. This is where the power of PowerPoint lies. You decide how and when each element appears on a slide. Remember, you must animate each slide separately. **Animate the other slides**. **Save** the presentation.

Start -
Automatically, On Mouse Click

Animation Tag -
Order it was animated

Event Order -
Lets you change the order in which the selected element appears

 **X and 2001 only**

This section is for PowerPoint X and 2001 users only. Users of other versions go to your section of this activity.

Adding Animations

1. **Double-click Slide 2** so it appears in full size.

2. Click the **Slide Show menu**, choose **Animations**, then **Custom**. Click the **Effects tab**.

3. Click **Object 3** in the **Select to animate** section. It becomes selected in the **Preview** section to show you the element you are working with.

4. Click the **arrow** in **Entry effect** and choose **Fly In From Left**.

5. Click **Text 2** in the **Select to animate** section.

6. Click the **arrow** in **Entry effect** and choose **Fly In From Right**.

7. Click the **arrow** in **Entry Sound** and choose **Whoosh**.

8. Click the **Order and Timing tab**.

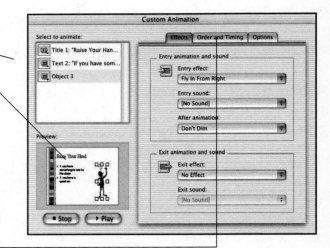

9. Click to select **Text 2**. In the **Start animation** section, **On mouse click** is selected. This is good because you will want to click the mouse to control when the text appears.

10. Click **Object 3**. In the **Start animation** section, click **Automatically** and type **1** in the seconds box.

11. Click the **Play button** to see the results.

12. With **Object 3** selected, click the **Down arrow** in the **Animation order** section. Click **Play** to see the change. Click the **Up arrow** to restore the order. Click **OK**.

13. Click the **Play button** in the lower left corner of the screen. Click the mouse to begin the animations where a mouse click was chosen. Press the **Esc** key to stop the show.

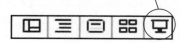

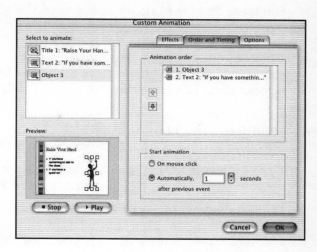

Animating the Remaining Slides

1. Scroll to Slide 3. Click the **Slide Show menu**, choose **Animations**, then **Custom**.

2. Click the **box to the left of Object 3** in the **Select to animate** section. The graphic becomes selected in the **Preview** section to show you the element you are working with.

3. Click the **Order and Timing tab**. Click the **arrow in Entry effect** and choose **Fly In From Right**. **Experiment with the buttons** to see what they do. This is where the power of PowerPoint lies. You decide how and when each element appears on a slide. Remember, you must animate each slide separately. **Animate the remaining slides. Save** the presentation.

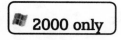 *This section is for PowerPoint 2000 users only. Users of other versions go to your section of this activity.*

Adding Animations

1. **Double-click Slide 2** so it appears in full size.

2. Click the **Slide Show menu**, and choose **Custom Animation**.

3. Click **Object 3** in the **Check to animate slide objects** section. The graphic becomes selected in the **Preview** section to show you the element you are working with. Checked objects will be animated.

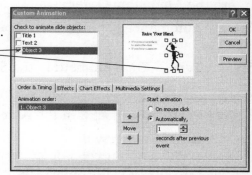

4. Click **Automatically** in the **Start animation** section. Type **1** in the **box**.

5. Click the **box to the left of Text 2** and then click **On mouse click** in the **Start animation** section. You will want to click the mouse to control when the text appears.

6. Click the **Effects** tab.

7. Click **Object 3** in the **Check to animate slide objects** section. In the **Entry animation and sound** section, choose **Fly** and **From Right** by clicking the **arrows**.

8. Click **Text 2** in the **Select to animate** section.

9. Choose **Fly** and **From Left** in the **Whoosh** as a **sound**.

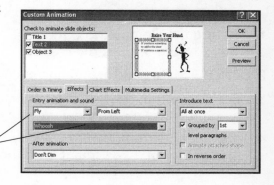

10. Click **the Preview** button to see how the slide is currently animated.

11. Click the **Order & Timing tab**.

12. **Click the up arrow** (located to the right of the Animation Order box). The Text element will move to the top indicating it will appear last. Click **Preview**. Using the arrows, **reset the order of appearance**. Click **Preview** to test it. Click **OK**.

Animating the Remaining Slides

1. Scroll to Slide 3. Click the **Slide Show menu** and choose **Custom Animation.**

2. Click **Object 3** in the **Select to animate** section. The graphic becomes selected in the **Preview** section to show you the element you are working with.

3. Click the **arrow** in **Entry effect** and choose **Fly In From Right. Experiment with the buttons** to see what they do. This is where the power of PowerPoint lies. You decide how and when each element appears on a slide. Remember, you must animate each slide separately. **Animate the remaining slides. Save** the presentation.

 *This section is for PowerPoint 98 and 97 users only.*
Users of other versions go to your section of this activity.

1. **Double-click Slide 2** so it appears in full size.

2. Click the **Slide Show** menu and choose **Custom Animation.**

3. Click the **Timing tab**. Click **Object 3** in the **Slide objects without animation** section. It moves from that section into the Animation order box. The graphic becomes selected in the **Preview** section to show you the element you are working with.

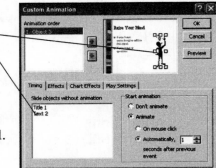

4. Click **Animate** in the **Start Animation section**. Object 3 moves up into the **Animation Order section** to show you it will be animated.

5. Click **Automatically** in the **Start Animation section**. Type **1** in the box.

6. Click **Text 2**. Click **Animate** in the **Start Animation section**. Click **On mouse click**.

7. Click the **Preview button** to see how the slide is currently animated.

8. Click the word **Object 3** in the **Animation Order** section.

9. Click the **down arrow** (located to the right of the Animation Order box). Text 2 moves to the top indicating it will appear first. Using the arrows, reset the order of appearance. Click **Preview** to test it. Click **OK.**

Animating the Remaining Slides

1. Scroll to **Slide 3. Click the graphic.**

2. Click the **Slide Show menu** and choose **Custom Animation.**

3. Click **Object 3** in the **Select to animate** section. The graphic becomes selected in the **Preview** section to show you the element you are working with.

4. Click the **Effect tab**, then the **arrow** in **Entry effect** and choose **Fly In From Right**. Click the **Preview button. Experiment with the buttons** to see what they do. This is where the power of PowerPoint lies. You decide how and when each element appears on a slide. Remember, you must animate each slide separately. **Animate the remaining slides. Save** the presentation.

Viewing Slides in the Notes Page View

1. **Scroll** to **Slide 2 Raise Your Hand**. Place the cursor on the raised line below the slide. When it turns into a crosshair (square on the Macintosh), drag the line up to make more typing room.

Users of earlier versions click the **Notes Page View** icon, or choose **Notes Page** from the **View** menu. An area for typing notes about the slide appears.

2. **Type the notes** below.

> 1. Wait until I call on you to speak.
> 2. I'll call on you in the order I see you raise your hand.
> 3. Please wait patiently until I call on you. Be a polite listener while you wait. Your classmates will do the same for you.

 *Don't click the **Print** icon. It will print each slide on a separate page!*

The slide show doesn't show the notes. You need to print the presentation to see the notes. Be sure to choose Notes Pages from the Print What menu in the Print dialog box.

Printing Notes Pages of the Slide Show Presentation

1. Press ⌨ (Windows) ⌨ (Macintosh) or choose **Print** from the **File** menu.

2. Click the **arrow** after the words **Print What**.

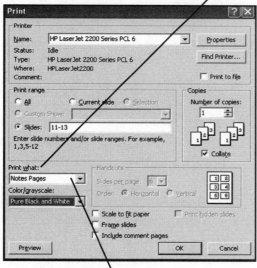

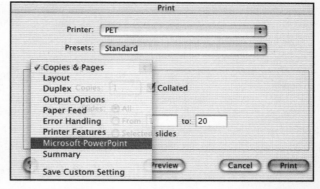

Macintosh users must first choose Microsoft PowerPoint from their print window before they see the PowerPoint options including Print What. Clicking the arrows next to the word General usually produces the option.

3. Drag to choose **Notes Pages**.

4. **Type "2"** in the **From** box, type **"2"** in the **To** box. Click **OK** or **Print**. This will print only page 2 (the only pages with notes).

 *Every page will be printed separately with notes below the slide. A blank space will appear if there are no notes. You may wish to choose the Notes Pages option for slides containing notes and print the rest (or all of the show) as handouts.*

Creating a Rain Forest Presentation with *HyperStudio*

HyperStudio is a software program that makes it easy to create nonlinear multimedia presentations. With *HyperStudio* you can build in links to create a presentation with branching pathways. Follow the steps below to build a simple presentation with *HyperStudio*.

Goal

To create a two-card multimedia presentation on the Tropical Rain Forest of South America with a live Internet link.

Get Started

1. Launch *HyperStudio 4*.

2. The Tip of the Day! stack opens that has handy notes on features. Take time later to explore these features. From the File menu, choose New Stack. After clicking OK, you will have a blank "Untitled" card to begin your stack.

3. Notice a blank white screen with the words "Untitled-Card 1" on the top.

You have just created a card and are on your way!

Creating a Text Object

1. Under Objects in the menu bar, choose Add a Text Object... to create a title for the first card. A window with text in it appears in the center of the card. Read the text carefully and then click OK.

2. A red-dotted rectangle (your future text object) has appeared on your card. Click and hold in the center of the red-dotted rectangle to move it to the left half of the card. Click and hold the red-dotted line to resize the rectangle. Have the rectangle fill the left half of the card.

3. After sizing the red-dotted rectangle, release the mouse button and click outside the rectangle (not on the red-dotted line). The Text Appearance window opens. Notice on the left side of the window that there are two color boxes.

Move your cursor to the top color box titled Text and click a red color (this will make your text appear red on the card).

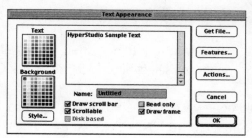 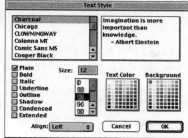

4. Move your cursor to the bottom color box titled Background and click a yellow color (this will make the background of the text object appear yellow on the card). Click the Style button directly below the Background color box.

5. A new window appears named Text Style. This is where you will create the look of the text on your card. Notice the number 12 is highlighted next to Size. In the box below, scroll down to select 36.

6. Use the Align pull-down menu and choose Center. This will center your text in your text box. Click OK.

7. Notice you are back in the Text Appearance window. We're almost done! Near the bottom of the window there are four small check boxes: Draw Scroll Bar, Scrollable, Read Only, and Draw Frame.

8. Click the Draw Scroll Bar, Scrollable, and Draw Frame check boxes to de-select them (remove the √) and then click OK. (All options will be de-selected.)

9. Let's get our tool bar on the desktop before we really get to work! From the Tools menu, click, hold and drag the tool bar onto your desktop. This is called a tear-away menu that allows you to easily access your tools.

10. Click the Browse tool  in the upper left of the tool bar. You cannot type unless your cursor looks like a hand. Look at the text object box. There is a long black blinking line near the top of the card. This line is called the cursor and it shows where you may begin typing. Type "Welcome to the South American Rain Forest."

Adding a Picture

1. From the File menu, choose Add Clip Art. A window will appear asking, "Where do you want to get your picture?" Click Disk File and then click OK.

2. In most cases *HyperStudio* will default you to a folder titled Media Library. Double-click Maps and then scroll down and select South America. Click Open.

3. A window titled Clip Art should open with the map of South America. Click Scale/Rotate and change the Scale factor to 75%. Click OK.

4. In the left corner of the clip art window there are two tools: a rectangle and a lasso. Double-click the Lasso tool. You should see red lines surrounding the map of South America. Click OK.

5. Notice that the map of South America has appeared on your card. Click and hold the mouse button somewhere in the center of the map and move it to the right side of your card (opposite your text object).

6. On your tool bar, click the Paint Bucket tool (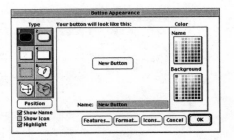). From the Colors menu, select the yellow that matches the background of the *text object*. (The color menu can be placed on the desktop by following the same directions used to move the tool bar.) After selecting the color, place the Paint Bucket on the white area of the card and click once.

How to Create and Connect to Another Card Using a Button

1. Under Objects in the menu bar, choose Add a Button... A window appears named Button Appearance.

2. In the text box next to Name where the words New Button appear high-lighted, type "Let's Go!" Choose the white rectangle shape (#3) and in the color box below Background, select a blue color. Click Format and choose a Font size of 18. Click OK and then OK again.

3. Notice that a window appears with text inside of it. Carefully read the text, and then click OK. Your new button appears in the middle of the card with a dotted red line around it. Just like you did with the picture, click and hold the mouse button down in the center of the Let's Go! button and place the button in the lower right corner of your card. Release the mouse and click outside the button and not on the red-dotted line.

4. A window appears titled Actions. Under Places to Go, click Another Card. A window appears asking you to move to the card to connect to. *However, in order to do this a new card must be created!*

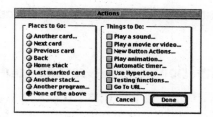

5. To create a new card, type Command (⌘) + N. You should see a new card appear. You'll know it's a new card because it is titled Untitled-Card 2 and the background is white. Click OK.

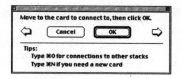

6. Next you need to pick a transition. Click Fade to Black and click Try It. Experiment with some other transitions and speeds by clicking on the transition and then Try It. Once you've found one you like, click OK.

Note: You will need a microphone on your computer to do the next step.

7. You are back in the window titled Actions. Under Things to Do, select Play a Sound. The Digital Audio Deck window opens. Click the green Record button and say *"Let's go to the South American Rain Forest."* When you are done speaking, click the Stop button. Click Play to hear the recording you made, then click OK.

8. You are back in the Actions window. Click Done. You should now be back on your card, and your cursor should now be the Browse tool. Click the Let's Go button. Your title card should transition into your second card.

Adding Text & Animations to Your Second Card

1. Follow the process outlined previously to add a text object to your second card. In the text object, write about the plants and animals that might be found in a tropical rain forest (i.e., parrots, monkeys, snakes, frogs, butterflies, kapok trees, rubber plants). This time do not de-select Draw Scroll Bar, Scrollable, and Draw Frame. You will now be able to type a lot of information into a small space and see the scrolling text box.

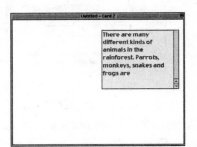

2. From Objects in the menu bar, choose Add a Button. Name your button Butterflies and click OK. Place your button near the bottom of the card and then click outside the button.

3. Under Things to Do, click Play Animation. Click Disk Library and then open the Animation folder. Select butterfly and click Open.

4. Notice your cursor is now a butterfly. Click and drag your mouse across the screen and press the Return/Enter key when finished. Click OK and then Done.

5. When you click your Butterflies button, you will see the butterfly float across the screen!

Adding an Internet Hyperlink to Your Second Card

1. Follow the first part of the process outlined previously to add a button to your second card. (When you get to the Actions window, follow the directions below.) Title your new button *Internet.*

2. Place the button near your text object, and then click outside of the button. A window titled Actions should appear. Under Things to Do, click the New Button Actions check box.

3. A window titled New Button Actions will appear. Under the box titled Names, scroll through the list until you find NetPage. Click NetPage. Click the button in the bottom left that says Use this NBA.

4. A new window will appear. In the box titled Uniform Resource Locator, type the following Web address: http://www.worldwildlife.org/amazon/sounds.htm. Click OK. Click OK in the next screen and then click Done in the Actions window.

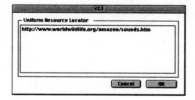

5. Test your new NetPage button by clicking it. Your Web browser should open and automatically load *Sights and Sounds of the Amazon.* Great work!

Tips and Troubleshooting

1. If your Web browser does not automatically open, try opening it while running *HyperStudio* (in the background). Click the NetPage button after your browser is open to test the button again.

2. Double-check that you typed the appropriate protocol (http://) before the URL and that the URL is correct.

3. *Save your stack immediately!* Choose Save Stack under File in the menu bar. Give your stack an easy-to-remember title.

4. Add new cards, buttons, and clip art to your stack by following the directions in this walkthrough.

5. Return to your first card by selecting First Card under Move in the menu bar.

6. See all of your cards at one time by selecting Storyboard from the Extras menu.

Creating a K-W-L Web with *Inspiration*

Inspiration is a powerful visual organization tool that students and teachers can use to develop ideas and organize their thinking graphically. Teachers and students use *Inspiration* for brainstorming, webbing ideas, and prewriting activities. You can easily switch back and forth between graphical view and a more traditional outline view of information.

Goal

To create a visual K-W-L (What We Know, What We Want to Know, and What We've Learned) web for a new theme unit on Dinosaurs.

Get Started

1. Launch *Inspiration*.

2. When you start *Inspiration*, you are in Diagram view. The Main Idea symbol appears in the center of your screen.

Create a Main Idea

Delete the words "Main Idea" and type "Dinosaurs." Notice that this becomes the main idea for your new visual plan.

Add Ideas to Your Diagram

1. Click the symbol outline of your main idea to highlight it. You will know it is highlighted when the symbol has red squares and diamonds around it.

2. From the Diagram toolbar at the top of the screen, click on the arrow pointing straight down in the Create Button.

3. In the new symbol that has just been created, type "What we KNOW about Dinosaurs."

Use RapidFire to Add Ideas Quickly

1. Click the "What we KNOW about Dinosaurs" symbol to highlight it.

2. From the Diagram toolbar, click the RapidFire button. Notice that a red lightning bolt appears next to the text.

3. Type "Are Extinct" and press the Return/Enter key on your keyboard. Notice that a new symbol linked to "What we KNOW about Dinosaurs" has been created.

4. While still in the RapidFire mode, type "Laid Eggs," "Some Ate Meat," and "Some Ate Plants." Be sure to press the Return/Enter key between each category!

5. Your diagram should resemble the one below:

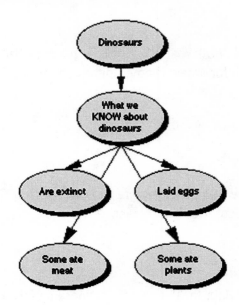

Change the Forms of Symbols

1. Click the "What we KNOW about Dinosaurs" symbol to highlight it.

2. On the left side of the screen is the Symbol Palette. If the palette is not visible, use the View menu to select Symbol Palette.

3. From the Symbol Palette, click the Central Arrow ▼ to see a list of the symbol graphic categories.

4. If Basic is not presently displayed, scroll to it. Click the picture of the light bulb and notice how the "What we KNOW about Dinosaurs" symbol changes.

Note: You can manually rearrange the symbols by clicking and dragging them to the desired location.

Add Information in Outline View

1. From the Diagram toolbar, click the Outline button. Notice that your visual plan has been arranged in outline format and that new buttons appear on the toolbar.

2. Click "Dinosaurs" and then click the Add Sub button on the Outline toolbar.

3. Type "What we WANT to know about Dinosaurs," click the Add Topic button, and then type "What we've LEARNED about Dinosaurs."

4. To put the three steps in order, click the roman numeral (III.) in front of "What we KNOW about Dinosaurs" and drag it to the top of the sub-topics under Dinosaurs. When you let go, it will become I.

5. Click the Diagram button on the Outline tool bar to return to Diagram view.

Change the Appearance of the Diagram Text

1. Highlight the "Dinosaurs" symbol. (You should see red squares and diamonds around the symbol.)

2. Use the Format menu to choose a new Font, Size, and Style for the text. (Try Chicago, 14, and Shadow.)

3. Use the Effect menu to change the Text Color. (You can also change the Fill Color and Line Color for the selected symbol using the Effect menu.)

4. Repeat the above steps for each symbol in your diagram. To change all of the symbols at the same time, choose Select All from the Edit menu and then follow steps 2 and 3.

Extensions

Want some great classroom ideas using *Inspiration*? Check out the *Inspiration* Web site at: **http://www.inspiration.com**

Visit the Tom Snyder Productions Web site to download a demo version of Graph Master *to use with this walk through.*
www.tomsnyder.com/weaving

Graphing Students' Favorite Fruits with
Graph Master

While programs like Microsoft *Excel* can help you create professional-looking graphs, *Graph Master* is a software program that is designed to help you teach graphing. After collecting and entering data, students select the variables, scale, and graph type appropriate for their data. The program's filter, sort, and compare features help students analyze data in different ways.

Below are instructions for creating a simple graph with *Graph Master.*

Goal

To create a graph containing collected data.

Get Started

Insert the *Graph Master* Demo CD and double-click the *Graph Master* Demo icon to begin. Click NEW Data Set.

Enter Data

We will begin by entering the following data containing student fruit choices.

Grade 5	Grade 6	Grade 7
apple 19	apple 12	apple 16
pear 5	pear 6	pear 3
banana 6	banana 15	banana 12
orange 10	orange 15	orange 6
plum 3	plum 0	plum 8

1. At the top of the data table, click the box containing the words "Variable A" and type "Fruit." Press Return/Enter on your keyboard to get to the first row. Type "apple," press Return/Enter again, and continue to label each row with the names of the fruit.

2. Click your cursor in the Variable B cell, click and type "Grade 5." Add the fruit data and then continue to add the rest of the information so that your completed table resembles the one on the next page.

	A	B	C	D
	Fruit	**Grade 5**	**Grade 6**	**Grade 7**
1	apple	19	12	16
2	pear	5	6	3
3	banana	6	15	12
4	orange	10	15	6
5	plum	3	0	8

3. From the Data menu, choose Show Column Totals. The total number of fruit for each grade level will appear at the bottom of the table.

Create a Graph

1.  Click the Graph button on the toolbar on the left side of your screen. The Choose Variables dialog box appears. Click the checkboxes next to Fruit and Grade 5, and then click OK. The Graph Type dialog box appears.

2. Click the highlighted graph types to see a description of each graph. Move your cursor over the gray boxes to read an explanation of why certain graphs are unavailable for this particular data set. Click Bar Graph, and then click OK.

3. The Set the Scale dialog box appears. The numbers in red show the range of data displayed on the y-axis. Type "25" in the box for the Maximum, "5" for the Step Size, and then click OK.

4. Click the word "Title" at the top of the bar graph, type "Grade 5 Survey," and then click OK.

5. Click the y-axis label (Grade 5), type "Number of Students," and then click OK.

6. From the Graphs menu bar, choose Change Colors... Click the red square on the color palette and then click the apple label. Change the colors for the rest of the labels, and then click OK.

Change Graph Type

1. At the top of the page, move your cursor slowly over each Graph Type button to see the names of the graphs.

2. Click the Circle Graph button.

3. Click one of the labels on the circle graph. Click the button for percent, and then click OK.

Analyze Graphs

1.  Click Data Table on the tool bar, and then click Graph. Click the checkbox next to Grade 5 to deselect it. Click the Grade 6 check box, and then click OK.

2. Click Circle Graph, and then click OK. Change the title to Grade 6 Survey.

3. Change the circle graph labels to percentages, and then change the colors to match the labels used in the Grade 5 Survey.

Note: If you've forgotten the colors and want to look at the Grade 5 Survey Graph, click Window List on the toolbar and then choose Grade 5 Survey.

4.  Click Compare on the toolbar. The Compare dialog box appears. Use the pull-down menu on the left to choose the first graph you created (Grade 5 Survey) and the pull-down menu on the right to choose the second graph. Click OK.

5.  Click Notebook on the toolbar. Write a few sentences describing the two graphs. Click the close box on the notebook when you are finished.

Printing Options

1. From the File menu bar, choose Print. Click Grade 5 Survey and Grade 6 Survey.

2. Experiment with the various print options and notice how they change in Preview. Click Cancel.

Extensions

1. Compare two circle graphs! Create a new circle graph containing Grade 5 Survey information. Label the graph using decimals or fractions and compare it to the Grade 5 Survey graph labeled with percentages. What can your students learn by comparing the two graphs?

2. Create a bar graph containing three variables! Click Graph and click the checkboxes for Fruit, Grade 6, and Grade 7. Have your students write questions about the data presented in this graph.

3. Analyze graphs created using different scales! Create two bar graphs containing Grade 7 information. Set the scale on one graph from 2 to 18 with a step size of 5, and the other from 2 to 30 with a step size of 5. How is the same information presented differently?

4. For some great ideas on using *Graph Master,* visit **http://www.tomsnyder.com/ classroom/graphmaster.**

5. How can you integrate *Graph Master* into your existing curriculum? Write your ideas below.

_____

_____

_____

_____

_____

Education and Technology Organizations

Visit the Tom Snyder Productions Web site at **www.tomsnyder.com/weaving** to find links to these organizations.

Association for Educational
Communications and Technology
(AECT)
1025 Vermont Avenue NW
Suite 820
Washington, DC 20005-3547
202-347-7834

Association of Supervision and
Curriculum Development (ASCD)
1703 Beauregard Street
Alexandria, VA 22311-1714
1-800-933-ASCD

Center for Children and
Technology (CCT)
Education Development Center, Inc.
96 Morton Street, 7th Floor
New York, NY 10014
212-807-4200

Computer Learning Foundation (CLF)
P.O. Box 60007
Palo Alto, CA 94306-0007
650-327-3347

International Society for
Technology in Education
480 Charnelton Street
Eugene, OR 97401-2626
1-800-336-5191

Institute for the Transfer of
Technology to Education
National School Boards Association
1680 Duke Street
Alexandria, VA 22314
703-838-6214

Technical Education Research
Center (TERC)
TERC has several telecommunica-
tions-based projects for science
and math, including Global Lab
and Lab Net.
2067 Massachusetts Avenue
Cambridge, MA 02140
617-547-0430

Triangle Coalition for Science
and Technology Education
1201 New York Avenue NW
Suite 700
Washington, DC 20005
1-800-582-0115

Education and Technology Publications

Visit the Tom Snyder Productions Web site at **www.tomsnyder.com/weaving** to find links to these publications.

Children's Software Revue
44 Main Street
Flemington, NJ 08822
908-284-0404

Classroom Connect (A guide to using the Internet)
Wentworth Worldwide Media, Inc.
P.O. Box 10488
Lancaster, PA 17605-0488
1-800-638-1639

Educational Software Preview Guide
Distributed by ISTE
1-800-336-5191

Electronic School
1680 Duke Street
Alexandria, VA 22314
703-838-6722

From Now On - The Educational Technology Journal
Network 609
500 15th Street
Bellingham, WA 98225
360-647-8759

InterActive Teacher
6990 Lake Ellenor Drive
Orlando, FL 32809
407-816-5420

Learning & Leading with Technology
published by the International Society for Technology in Education
1-800-336-5191

Media & Methods
1429 Walnut Street
Philadelphia, PA 19102
215-563-6005

Multimedia Schools
143 Old Marlton Pike
Medford, NJ 08055-8750
609-654-6266

Online - Offline
Rock Hill Press
14 Rock Hill Road
Bala Cynwyd, PA 19004
610-661-2040

Technological Horizons in Education (T.H.E.) Journal
150 El Camino Real, Suite 112
Tustin, CA 92780-3670
714-730-4011

Technology & Learning
P.O. Box 5052
Vandalia, OH 45377
1-800-607-4410

Technology Connection
Linworth Publishing, Inc.
480 East Wilson Bridge Road, Suite L
Worthington, OH 43085-2372
614-436-7107

Recommended Reading List

Anderson, Charnel. *Technology in American Education, 1650–1900.* Washington, DC: GPO, 1962.

Bruner, Jerome. *Acts of Meaning.* Cambridge: Harvard University Press, 1990.

Center for Science, Mathematics, and Engineering Education, National Research Council. *Inquiry and the National Science Education Standards: A Guide for Teaching and Learning.* Washington, DC: National Academy Press, 2000.

Classroom Ideas Using Inspiration: For Teachers by Teachers. Portland, OR: Inspiration Software, Inc., 1998.

Cuban, Larry. *How Teachers Taught: Constancy and Change in American Classrooms,* 1890–1990. New York: Teachers College Press, 1993.

Cuban, Larry. *Oversold and Underused: Computers in Classrooms, 1980–2000.* Cambridge, MA: Harvard University Press, 2001.

Cuban, Larry. *Teachers and Machines.* New York: Teachers College Press, 1986.

Dockterman, David A. and Tom Snyder. *Bringing the Computer into Your Classroom.* Cambridge, MA: Tom Snyder Productions, 1987.

Dockterman, David A. *Tools for Teachers: An Historical Analysis of Classroom Technology.* Doctoral thesis, Harvard Graduate School of Education, 1988.

Egan, Keiran. *Teaching as Storytelling: An Alternative Approach to Teaching and Curriculum.* Chicago: Chicago University Press, 1989.

Egan, Keiran. *Imagination in Teaching & Learning.* Chicago: University of Chicago Press, 1992.

Freedman, Samuel. *Small Victories.* New York: Harper & Row, 1989.

Gordon, David T., ed. *The Digital Classroom: How Technology Is Changing the Way We Teach and Learn.* Cambridge, MA: President and Fellows at Harvard University, 2000.

Grant, Gerald and Christine Murray. *Teaching in America: The Slow Revolution.* Cambridge, MA: Harvard University Press, 1999.

Hampel, Robert L. *The Last Little Citadel: American High Schools Since 1940.* Boston: Houghton Mifflin Company, 1986.

Herndon, James. *Notes from a Schoolteacher.* New York: Simon and Schuster, 1985.

Jackson, Philip W. *The Teacher and the Machine.* Pittsburgh: University of Pittsburgh Press, 1968.

Kidder, Tracy. *Among Schoolchildren.* Boston: Houghton Mifflin Company, 1989.

Kohn, Alfie. *The Schools Our Children Deserve.* New York: Mariner Books, 2000.

Lakoff, George and Mark Johnson. *Metaphors We Live By.* Chicago: University of Chicago Press, 1982.

Leu, Donald J. and Deborah Diadiun Leu. *Teaching with the Internet: Lessons from the Classroom.* Norwood, MA: Christopher-Gordon Publishers, 2000.

Meeting Standards with Inspiration: Core Curriculum Lesson Plans. Portland, OR: Inspiration Software, Inc., 1999.

Murnane, Richard and Frank Levy. *Teaching the New Basic Skills.* New York: The Free Press, 1996.

Neustadt, Richard E. and Ernest R. May. *Thinking in Time.* New York: St. Martin's Press, 1981.

Oettinger, Anthony G. *Run, Computer, Run. The Mythology of Educational Innovation.* Cambridge, MA: Harvard University Press, 1969.

Papert, Seymour. *Mindstorms.* New York: Basic Books, 1980.

Papert, Seymour. *Children's Machine: Rethinking School in the Age of the Computer.* New York: Basic Books, 1993.

Parker Roerden, L. *Net Lessons: Web-Based Projects for Your Classroom.* Sebastopol, CA: Songline Studios, 1997.

Perelman, Lewis. *School's Out.* New York: William Morrow, 1992.

Postman, Neil. *The End of Education.* New York: Alfred A. Knopf, 1995.

Powell, Arthur G., Eleanor Farrar, and David K. Cohen. *The Shopping Mall High School.* Boston: Houghton Mifflin Company, 1985.

Saettler, Paul. *A History of Educational Technology.* New York: McGraw-Hill Book Company, 1968.

Sarason, Seymour. *The Predictable Failure of Educational Reform.* San Francisco: Jossey-Bass, 1990.

Sizer, Theodore. *Horace's Compromise.* Boston: Houghton Mifflin Company, 1985.

Snyder, Tom and David Dockterman. "Getting to Aha!" in *Electronic Learning,* Vol. 3, No. 8, 1983.

Snyder, Tom and Jane Palmer. *In Search of the Most Amazing Thing.* Reading, MA: Addison-Wesley Publishing Company, Inc., 1986.

Vygotsky, Lev S. *Thought and Language.* Cambridge: MIT Press, 1986.

Weizenbaum, Joseph. *Computer Power and Human Reason.* San Francisco: W. H. Freeman and Company, 1976.